TURNING
SALT & PEPPER
SHAKERS AND MILLS

TURNING
SALT & PEPPER
SHAKERS AND MILLS

CHRIS WEST

Foreword by GARY RANCE

GUILD OF MASTER
CRAFTSMAN PUBLICATIONS

First published 2011 by
Guild of Master Craftsman Publications Ltd
Castle Place, 166 High Street, Lewes,
East Sussex BN7 1XU

ISBN: 978-1-86108-825-3

Publisher: Jonathan Bailey
Production Manager: Jim Bulley
Managing Editor: Gerrie Purcell
Project Editor: Judith Chamberlain-Webber
Editor: Stephen Haynes
Managing Art Editor: Gilda Pacitti
Designer: Rob Janes

Set in Frutiger, Optimus Princeps, and Timeless
Color origination by GMC Reprographics
Printed and bound by Hung Hing Offset Ltd

FOREWORD

As someone who started his working life turning salt and pepper mills, and who has continued to turn them ever since, I am fully aware of the need for a book like this. You would never believe the number of problems that can arise from creating such a well-loved piece of kitchen equipment and ensuring that each pair is a perfect match. A well-turned pepper mill has many roles in addition to its obvious use as a means of grinding pepper—as an ornament, for example, or an icebreaker for nervous dinner guests.

Chris West has been designing and turning mills for the last 12 years, which is unusual for someone who is not a full-time woodturner. In this book he offers techniques and styles ranging from the traditional to the contemporary. He encourages you to think laterally when designing mills, and shows you where to look for inspiration. Chris also provides all the technical information you need about the mechanisms and other accessories that can be incorporated into your mills, whether the design is traditional or from your own imagination.

This book is well overdue in that it helps take away the fear that some woodturners have about turning condiment holders.

GARY RANCE

Contents

INTRODUCTION

The best way to start woodturning is to take a class with a qualified instructor. That way, you begin your career without any bad habits.

I started woodturning in the 1970s, using a power drill and lathe attachment. My tools were scrapers made from old files. I can see you cringing already! Ignorance is bliss—I had the confidence of youth and few thoughts about safety. Now, in my senior years, I have access to turning tools made of properly tempered tool steel, and if I need to fashion a tool for a specific job, I try to make it from one of these. The pole-lathe turners of the past did not allow the restrictions of their simple tools to stop them from designing and turning lovely pieces. The brief history of shakers and mills on pages 26–29 will help you to appreciate the skills and craftsmanship of the pole-lathe turner.

My background in precision engineering (see page 172) is one of the many reasons why I love designing and turning shakers and mills. When I see something attractive, I make a mental note of its basic shape, though it is often some time later that I commit it to paper and adapt it for a specific project. The resulting sketch will usually look quite different from the original object I saw in the gallery or store, and that's all to the good. I wouldn't want to just copy someone else's design—and in any case, with my memory, there's very little chance of my sketch being the same. Wherever possible, for each project in this book I have included details of how to adapt the same design to suit different accessories or different means of assembly, such as laminating. After all, not everyone has access to particular machinery, tools, or skills. But, I have assumed a basic level of turning ability and the availability of a chuck with expansion and compression jaws.

I have rated the projects as suitable for beginners, intermediate, or experienced woodturners. I must stress that the term "experienced" refers not just to your turning skills, but also assumes that you have access to the materials or machinery required for the project. I felt the need to include these more ambitious projects to encourage you to learn new skills.

It is very important to understand the range of accessories available to you (see pages 34–37 and 70–77). This information opens up a wide range of design possibilities, and you will soon find that there is very little you can't do when designing a shaker or mill. I cannot overemphasize how important it is that after reading this section you allow your mind to run free and be inspired.

There are some areas of turning that are not covered in detail in this book, such as thread chasing, texturing, and coloring. There are several excellent books available that can give you the guidance you need to take your designs into these new fields (see page 171). I would encourage you to explore these aspects of turning.

In the Projects sections I have included a number of shakers as well as mills. Poor old shakers are given little thought. If you belong to a woodturning club, how many times have you seen a salt and pepper shaker set in the gallery?

I have heard numerous turners say, "I must get around to turning a salt and pepper mill." After reading this book, I hope you will be able to say, "I want to turn not just one of these projects, but new designs I've thought of myself."

So, read the book and either turn some of the projects I have included or use the information given to produce your own designs. It is said that good design stands the test of time—good luck!

TECHNIQUES
AND
MATERIALS

HEALTH AND SAFETY

Are you one of those people who buys a new gadget, unpacks it, and immediately starts putting it together—and ends up with two or three extra pieces? If the answer is yes, don't worry—you are not alone.

You look for the instructions, only to find that they have been translated by a person who has limited knowledge of English and is relying on the pictures to tell you how it all goes together. You throw away the instructions and start to use your common sense instead.

Common sense—that's what health and safety is all about. Using a lathe and associated accessories is all about taking your time and *thinking* before doing something. While most of the points detailed on the opposite page are obvious, some have been learned by experience, so please take a few minutes to read through them carefully. They will enable you to enjoy woodturning in the safest possible way.

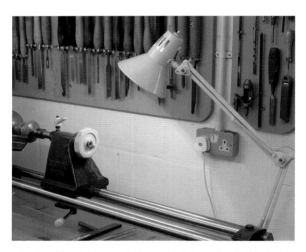

Good task lighting is essential for any kind of woodwork. This should include an adjustable light source near the lathe

A modern full-face helmet with respirator offers the best possible protection for face and lungs

It is advisable to wear safety glasses and a dust mask to protect yourself from the shavings and wood dust that are created when using a lathe

▶ BEFORE STARTING THE LATHE:

- Never use a lathe if you have recently had an alcoholic drink.

- Ensure you have good lighting in your workshop.

- Make sure you are dressed safely: loose sleeves, ties, long hair, and jewelry can get caught in the lathe when it is in motion.

- Wear safety glasses that include side protectors—or, better still, a full-face shield.

- In dusty work conditions, use a dust mask or helmet, and a proper ventilation and dust-collection system.

- Check that the jaws can't fall out of the chuck.

- Before mounting the wood on the lathe, examine it carefully for splits and cracks. Be aware of any bark and/or knots that are present (avoid these altogether if you are inexperienced), and take into consideration any irregularities in the shape of the wood.

- Ensure that the tool rest is firmly locked in place.

- Rotate the piece by hand to ensure that it is running clear of the tool rest and bed.

- Take care to avoid distractions, especially sudden ones such as someone coming into your view unexpectedly.

- Be aware that certain woods may cause skin irritation in some individuals.

▶ WHEN TURNING:

- If possible, always use the tailstock to steady the work, even on faceplate work that is secured by screws.

- Always start a new piece at a slow speed until the wood is in balance.

- Stop the lathe and check the equipment if you detect strange sounds or vibrations, or anything that does not seem right to you. You know the sounds of your vehicle; learn the sounds of your lathe.

- Sand the wood at the point where it is turning away from you.

- Always use paper towels or a safety cloth when applying finishes. Any other fabric could drag your hand into the work if it catches.

- Never leave the lathe running unattended. Turn it off.

- Remember that dust and shavings are a potential fire hazard.

Always hold sandpaper in such a way that it will be torn harmlessly out of your hand if it snags

TOOLS

The projects described in this book require only a modest number of tools, and most of them are not highly specialized. If you need basic advice on what equipment to buy, there are some excellent books available that cover the subject in much greater detail than is possible here. Product reviews in woodworking magazines may be helpful.

THE LATHE

Since I started out in the 1970s, I have traveled a route familiar to all turners. You outgrow your first lathe, move on to the next, and after a while you set your sights on the perfect lathe, which will be capable of turning just about anything you wish. The problem is, which comes first: the house loan, the growing family, or your hobby? For most of us, the ideal lathe, ancillary equipment, and tools have to take a back seat for a while.

So which lathe should you buy? The full list of criteria is too long to discuss here, but one feature that I have found very useful is variable speed capability. The lathe's diameter over the bed is important if you want to turn platters and bowls, and for pepper mills the length of the bed needs to be considered.

LATHE MAINTENANCE

Whichever lathe you own, proper maintenance will extend its lifespan. Keep the bed of the lathe clean and lightly oiled, allowing free movement of the tool rest base. The top edge of the tool rest must be kept smooth and level to allow free movement of the tools over it.

CHUCKS

Since most of us cannot afford numerous different chuck bodies, it is important to choose one for which a good number of different jaws are available. In the projects in this book there

A four-jaw scroll chuck fitted with small expansion jaws

are many instances when you need to switch between expansion and compression jaws, and sometimes different sizes are required. I recommend a scroll chuck. If you can buy an extended chuck key for it, all the better for tightening up the jaws, ensuring that the wood stays in place.

DRILLS

Sawtooth bits are used extensively in this book. For sizes over 1 in. (25 mm) in diameter I usually use imperial sizes (given in inches), but the metric equivalent size is also given in the text (in millimeters). From 1 in. (25 mm) down to $^{13}/_{32}$ in. (10 mm), I tend to use metric bits.

A sawtooth bit held in a Jacobs chuck; the drilling depth is indicated on the masking tape applied to the drill shank

A 1 in. (25 mm) sawtooth bit mounted in an extension for mills over 12 in. (305 mm) tall

From top to bottom (lower three items): twist drill with depth mark on masking tape; 1/16 in. (1.5 mm) drill for salt and pepper exit holes, mounted in a miniature Jacobs chuck; spur-point drill

Sawtooth bits, with saw-like teeth ground into the rim, are great for drilling 90° holes. The rim teeth cut, rather than score the wood, generating less heat and allowing a faster feed rate than knife-edge bits such as Forstner bits. Because it can handle a higher rim speed, the sawtooth style is most common on bits larger than 1 in. (25 mm) diameter.

Forstner bits are more suitable for cross-grain drilling; they are likely to heat up when drilling deep holes.

If you plan to turn a mill over 12 in. (305 mm) high, a sawtooth cutter shank extension is required. These usually add 6 in. (150 mm) to the maximum drilling depth.

When drilling deep holes, it is advisable to keep the bit sharp. This makes it easier on the lathe, and on the bit, and makes it easier to wind in the tailstock. Fine diamond files are recommended to keep the original angles and edges.

For holes under 3/8 in. (9.5 mm) diameter, spur bits and twist drills are used. The spur bits are useful because of their ability to give a clean-sided cut. Engineering twist bits have to be used for drilling very small holes such as the exit holes for salt and pepper shakers.

JACOBS CHUCK

All of these bits are held in the tailstock by a Jacobs chuck. I tend to use two sizes: one to hold bits up to 3/8 in. (9.5 mm), and a 1/2 in. (13 mm) one for the sawtooth bits.

TURNING TOOLS

The turning tools required are listed at the beginning of each project, so you can tell at a glance whether you have what you need.

CHISELS AND GOUGES

For salt and pepper shakers and mills I use the following basic set of tools:

- Spindle roughing gouges: 3/4 in. (19 mm) and 1 in. (25 mm)
- Spindle gouges: 3/8 in. (10 mm), 1/2 in. (13 mm)
- Parting tools: 1/16 in. (1.5 mm), 1/8 in. (3 mm), and a 3/8 in. (10 mm) beading and parting tool.

From top to bottom: beading and parting tool, thin parting tool, fluted parting tool, homemade recess tool, skew chisel, spindle gouge, spindle roughing gouge

SCRAPERS

The scrapers I use most are round-nosed; they range from the ⅛ in. (3 mm) miniature through to the ½ in. (13 mm) scraper. Occasionally I use a 1 in. (25 mm) square-end scraper.

SPECIAL TOOLS

A key tool in this category is the recess tool, also known as a relief-cutting tool, for use in thread chasing. It has a ³⁄₁₆ in. (5 mm) cutting edge for turning the recess at the bottom of the female thread. I also use it for cutting a ¼ in. (6 mm) slot for the three lugs on the CrushGrind® mechanisms, though at the time of writing I understand that a tool is being produced by Robert Sorby specifically for this job.

Hand thread chasers come in a number of sizes. For use with shakers, choose a set with around 19 teeth per inch (tpi). I use a homemade armrest, similar to that used by veteran turner Bill Jones, to support both the recess tool and the thread chaser.

You may be nervous about using a spindle gouge to produce a fine finishing cut at the point where a concave curve meets a convex curve. An alternative is to use a sharp, ½ in. (13 mm) half-round scraper to achieve the clean finish required.

SHARPENING CHISELS AND GOUGES

There are numerous grinders on the market. Choose one with a minimum 1 in. (25 mm) stone, which is of the highest quality. To assist you in sharpening the gouges, a sharpening jig is a good investment; it will give a consistent grind and shape to your gouges, and saves grinding too much steel away.

Most grinders come with an adjustable table and will help with the job of sharpening scrapers. The one I use incorporates both an adjustable table and a swiveling tool holder to give me the angles required for gouges.

A half-round scraper in action

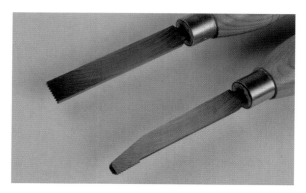

Male and female thread chasers

After a while, your grinding stone's surface will become concave. A wheel dresser is something you should purchase if you want to continue to get the correct angles and shapes on all of your tools.

BANDSAW

Along with the grinder, the one piece of equipment I consider almost essential for turning salt and pepper mills is a bandsaw. It does not have to be of industrial size, but one that will happily cope with wood approximately 4–5 in. (100–125 mm) thick. Mine is a floor-standing model. The blade I use most is ½ in. (13 mm) wide, 4 tpi, with skip teeth, which are great for general cutting.

THICKNESS PLANER

I do not possess a thickness planer for reasons of cost and space. However, a furniture-making friend allows me to use his, if I do the odd piece of "round work" for him. This is the kind of friendship I would encourage you to foster!

TERMINOLOGY

The following specialized terms are used throughout this book:

Combo mill

This is a combined salt shaker and pepper mill.

Condiment holder

Refers to a container that dispenses either salt or pepper.

CrushGrind®

Refers to either CrushGrind® shaft or CrushGrind® wood mechanisms (see page 73).

Finial nut

The nut supplied with the mechanism for holding the mill together. Also known as an adjustment knob or knurled knob.

Grinder

A word often used in North America to describe a completed turned condiment holder for grinding salt or pepper.

Grinding mechanism

The stainless steel or plastic assembly through which the aluminum shaft (or stem) of the mechanism passes.

ID plug

An insert of contrasting wood used at the top of a condiment holder to identify its contents—salt or pepper.

Insert nut

A nut with the same thread size as the shaft of a traditional grinding mechanism, used as an integral part of a finial nut designed by a woodturner. Also known as a dogtooth nut.

Reservoir

The cylinder or drilled hole within the body of the condiment holder that contains the salt or pepper.

Spigot

A term used for a turned section at the base of the top section of the mill, which fits into the top of the main body. Often called a tenon (or tongue in the UK).

Tenon

A cylindrical projection formed on a shaker or mill blank, enabling it to be held in compression jaws. This will, in most cases, be removed before the shaker or mill is completed. Often called a spigot in the UK.

Type 1 mechanism

My term for Cole & Mason® (UK) mechanisms.

Type 2 mechanism

My term for Chef Specialty® (USA) mechanisms.

Woods

A little time spent choosing the wood for your project can greatly enhance the design and quality of the end result. Use of contrasting woods can be especially effective.

When I receive commissions for a pair of shakers or mills, the client rarely has a clear idea of which wood to choose. Wherever you are in the world, the choice of woods available nowadays is extensive.

Are you going to leave the condiment holder natural? Is it to be oiled, sprayed with an acrylic finish, coated with polyurethane, or colored? Knowing which finish you are going to use will help in your choice of wood.

Whichever wood you choose, it must be dry. If it is not, the finished mill can turn oval, and the spigot will jam inside the main body, making it unusable.

Try to avoid wood that has large knots in it, unless you feel that the knot will enhance the end result. Branch wood can be turned into mills, but I would advise you to be wary. As with wet wood, there is a risk of the wood moving after completion because of inbuilt stresses.

Because we are making items associated with food, it is essential to avoid woods considered to be toxic. Also, many woods cause adverse reactions in turners, either in the form of external irritation or internal problems.

One wood I have used in the projects is yew. Despite the fact that the living tree is toxic, and the leaves and berries are poisonous, I have not seen any conclusive evidence to suggest that dry wood should not be used for shakers or mills.

I have also used spalted beech. Spalting is part of the decay process and is caused by fungus attacking the tree. Dust particles from the wood contain the spores of the fungus, which can affect the respiratory system, but the worked wood is unlikely to cause problems.

All wood produces fine particles of dust when worked, so, regardless of the wood you are using, good ventilation, dust extraction, and face masks must be considered an integral part of your working process.

On the following pages are details of the woods I have used in this book. Unless otherwise stated, they all turn well and a good finish can be obtained if the correct process is followed. There are many woods not listed that would be equally suitable; it's worth finding out about those that are native to your own country.

WOODS USED IN THE PROJECTS

European sycamore *(Acer pseudoplatanus)*
A weed to some, but a very usable wood to turners. European sycamore is a species of maple, and has similar qualities to other maples. It is a close and mostly straight-grained wood, creamy in color. In the UK, some turners regard it as a bland-grained wood and it is often colored. Grows throughout Europe.

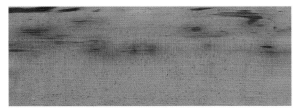

Boxwood *(Buxus sempervirens)*
A heavy, hard, and very fine-grained wood, usually white or creamy in color. Variations of the *Buxus* family can be found around the world. I also use boxwood as a contrasting insert for the identification of a salt shaker. Origin: Europe and North America.

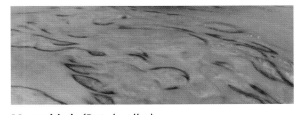

Masur birch *(Betula alba)*
The term *masur* refers not to a separate species of birch, but to a distinctive figure caused by insect attack. Lovely wood to turn, creamy in texture with dark brown flecks throughout. Origin: Russia and Scandinavia.

European sweet chestnut *(Castanea sativa)*
Very similar working properties to ash *(Fraxinus excelsior)*, but a little softer when turning. More brown than ash, more akin to oak. It is enhanced by lovely wavy grain patterns. Origin: Europe; related species are found in North America.

Satiné bloodwood *(Brosimum paraense)*
Known as *satiné* because of its high luster when finished, it is a very dense and hard wood with a tight grain. It is bright red in color—the nearest wood I know to blood-red. Origin: Brazil, Panama, Peru, and Venezuela.

East Indian rosewood *(Dalbergia latifolia)*
Also known as *sonokeling*. A tight-grained wood that lends itself to thread chasing. Its heartwood varies in color from rich rose to dark brown, and contains purplish-black. It is an oily wood but dusty when sanded. Origin: India.

Ebony *(Diospyros crassiflora)*
A hard, tight-grained wood renowned for its finishing capabilities. Black, sometimes with brown stripes. When turning, it can be brittle, so sharp tools are required. Origin: western Africa.

Pau amarello *(Euxylophora paraensis)*
This wood is known as yellowheart in North America. Very yellow in color. I use it mainly as a contrasting insert for identification of a salt shaker. Origin: Brazil.

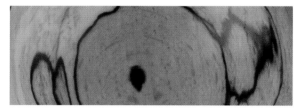

Spalted beech *(Fagus sylvatica)*
Beech is a dense, hard wood with an even grain. Spalting is a discoloration caused by fungal attack; it is the first stage in decay, and sometimes the wood can become soft or rotten. No two pieces are the same. Origin: UK, central Europe, western Asia.

Ash (American, *Fraxinus americana;* European, *F. excelsior*)
European ash is an open-grained wood ideal for ebonizing and gilding. Creamy in color, it often has areas of brown in it. European ash has a more wavy grain pattern than its American cousin, which also has a more yellowish or greenish tinge to it, and is softer to turn than European ash. Ash is found throughout Europe, North America, and Asia.

European walnut *(Juglans regia)*
European walnut has a grain that is lovely to look at and to work with. The heartwood is mid-brown. Known for fabulous figure that would enhance any mill—if you can find it. Origin: Europe and some parts of Asia.

Zebrano *(Microberlinia brazzavillensis)*
Creamy in color, with streaks of dark brown to black throughout the heartwood. Sometimes it feels soft to turn, and, as long as you don't mind the aroma when turning it, is a wood that is well worth considering. Origin: west Africa, Cameroon, Gabon.

Wengé *(Millettia laurentii)*
A dense wood, dark chocolate in color with light yellow streaks. It is a "gritty" wood to turn and the dust is very fine. Straight-grained and useful for ID plugs indicating pepper. Origin: Cameroon, Tanzania, Congo, Gabon, and other African countries.

Mulberry *(Morus nigra)*
A medium-density hardwood with a closed, straight grain, mulberry has a bright yellow sapwood with a light tan heartwood. It tends to turn brown with exposure to sunlight. Origin: Asia, South America, and southern parts of North America. In the UK it is mostly found in gardens and parks.

Olivewood *(Olea europaea)*
Olivewood has dark brown streaks among the yellowish-brown heartwood. It also has some lovely wavy patterns, which give your pieces the "wow" factor. I regard it as an oily wood. It is hard, but not difficult to turn. Origin: southern Europe and northern Africa.

Beli *(Paraberlinia bifoliolata)*
Similar to zebrano, without the unpleasant aroma. The streaks of dark brown to black are slightly narrower. Turns well and makes attractive mills. Origin: Cameroon and Gabon.

Pink ivory *(Rhamnus zeyheri)*
A rare and expensive wood: use sparingly! Its name implies its color, pink to red. Very hard with a tight grain. Origin: primarily South Africa.

False acacia or locust *(Robinia pseudoacacia)*
When turned, this wood is yellow-brown. After a time it will turn to a rich brown color. It turns easily and has very attractive markings. Origin: mostly North America.

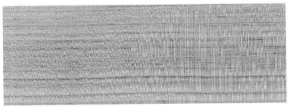

Cherry (American, *Prunus serotina;* European, *P. avium)*
A quite tight grain, orange in color, but turns darker over time. European cherry has a more wavy grain than the American variety. They both turn well. Origin: Cherry grows throughout Europe and North America.

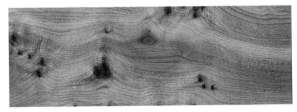

Yew *(Taxus baccata)*
Yew is reddish-brown in color, which in time turns to a lovely orange-brown. It has a tendency to develop crack lines if the lathe is running too fast during sanding. Origin: UK and Europe; there is a related species in North America.

European oak *(Quercus robur)*
Oak has an open texture and can be found in varying shades of brown. It darkens with age and has a lovely patina. Looks attractive when limed. Origin: Europe and north-eastern United States.

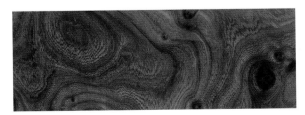

English elm *(Ulmus procera)*
This wood has a lovely mid-brown color. Can be "gritty" when turning. Lovely markings. The burrs are beautiful, if you can get them. Origin: northern Europe.

FINISHING

Three things make an attractive piece of turning: the shape, the wood, and the finish. Condiment holders receive a good deal of handling, so they need a durable finish.

Time spent on finishing will make the difference between a condiment holder that is merely satisfactory, and one that looks and feels wonderful. In my opinion, finishing begins with the last cut with the gouge or skew chisel.

SANDING

Your choice of sanding cloth is a matter of personal preference. Cloth-backed aluminum-oxide paper serves most of my sanding needs. For particular woods I will sometimes add either an oil or a paste wax to help lubricate the paper and reduce clogging. With most woods I start with 180-grit paper and work my way to 400-grit. If your lathe has reversing capabilities, reversing between grits can give a smoother finish. On smooth surfaces, I stop the lathe after each grit and sand horizontally with the grain. Throughout sanding, the speed of the lathe is around 500 rpm.

COLORING

Excellent books have been written on the subject of coloring wood, so I do not intend to cover it in detail here. Ebonizing and gilt cream are used in one of the projects (see page 98), so I will include the method used here.

After final shaping, sand down through the grits to 400, until you are satisfied that there are no sanding marks left. Now brush along the grain using a bronze brush. To ebonize the main body, the lathe will be turned by hand. Cover the bed, chuck, and any other exposed areas of your lathe to ensure that the ebonizing lacquer does not

stain your equipment. Spray horizontally in one continuous sweep. Turn the base a quarter turn by hand and repeat until the main body has been totally covered. Depending on your workshop's ambient temperature, the lacquer will take around 20 minutes per coat to dry. Using a soft cotton cloth, apply the gilt cream to the body in a circular motion to ensure that all parts of the softer summer growth are filled. The gilt cream will dry quite quickly. Use finishing or mineral oil to remove the excess gilt cream. Finally, buff the body. When the finishing oil has hardened (allow 24 hours for this), additional coats can be added or a gloss acrylic lacquer can be sprayed on to give it some further protection.

LETTERING

Contrasting woods are often used to differentiate between salt and pepper condiment holders. Another method is to have the words inscribed on the wood. There are several ways of doing this:

Lasering

LASERING

Usually a computer-generated JPEG file of the letters and design will be required for the laser-cutting machine. One disadvantage of this method is that the laser head is at a fixed height and the depth of cut will be reduced as the curved wood surface recedes from it.

ENGRAVING

Many local companies can do this. Engraving has an advantage over laser cutting in that the engraving cutter is physically in contact with the wood and will easily cope with a cylindrical surface.

Engraving

Decal

PYROGRAPHY

If you have a steady hand and an artistic inclination you may wish to burn the lettering onto the mill yourself.

With any of the three methods mentioned so far, the lettering can be blackened afterwards with a fine, permanent felt-tipped pen.

DECALS

Computer-generated lettering can be printed on inkjet printers using a dry rub-off decal paper (see page 168 for a worldwide supplier). Seal the wood surface before applying the decal; acrylic lacquer can then be sprayed over the lettering to protect it from being rubbed off.

SEALING

The basis of a waterproof finish is a mixture of 50% cellulose sealer and cellulose thinners. It is best applied by brush and will dry very quickly. I usually apply two coats, wiping off excess sealer with a clean paper towel. After the last coat of sealer and before any more finishing product is applied, rub over the rotating condiment holder with a white synthetic finishing pad to remove "nibs" of sealer. The Webrax pad (see pages 168–169 for suppliers) is made from aluminum-oxide or silicone-carbide grains, which adhere to a non-woven mix of nylon fibers.

DEFECTS

You will occasionally find that a particularly attractive piece of wood you wish to use has small cracks; yew is prone to these. Cyanoacrylate (Super Glue®) can be used to fill the cracks. It comes in three consistencies: thin, medium, and thick. Usually the thin or the medium will be suitable, depending on the size of the void to be filled. The hole or crack is first filled with matching wood dust. Once dry, the crack is hand-sanded to start with, before sanding with the lathe switched on. I would not recommend that you try speeding the process by using a quick-drying accelerator. This may cause a white haze on the surface, so be patient!

Occasionally, especially with spalted wood, there may be an area in which the rotting process has progressed to the point that the wood is soft. Assuming that the area is not too large, an application of wood hardener may well save a nice piece of wood from the firewood pile. Areas that have been hardened will sand well and take a spray finish as normal.

OIL

Oily woods such as rosewood and olive lend themselves to an oiled finish. Both Danish and finishing oil are suitable, but patience is required for any oil application. If possible, leave the oiling process until the end of the day and allow to dry overnight. De-nib the surface between coats. Leave the piece for a few days before progressing to the buffing process.

Most commercially available salt and pepper shakers and mills do not have a finish on the inside of the reservoir. If you are worried about this, consider lining the reservoir with a plastic tube. Alternatively, coat the inside with a barrier or a certified salad-bowl oil finish. Certification for food-safe finishes varies from country to country, but suitable products will be clearly labeled as food- or toy-safe.

Defects in the wood can be fixed with cyanoacrylate

Allow plenty of time for the oiling process

SPRAYING

All of my non-oily woods receive several coats of acrylic gloss lacquer. Spraying can be carried out while the condiment holder is still on the lathe, but because of time constraints I usually spray away from the lathe in a dust-free and well-ventilated area of the workshop.

Acrylic lacquer will, subject to the ambient temperature, be dry in 20 minutes. I recommend that the mill parts are put back on the lathe when dry to receive a de-nibbing between coats. The end result will be well worth the extra time. Usually a maximum of three coats will suffice.

I like to leave the sprayed items overnight before beginning the buffing process. I find that this "hardening" time gives me a better end result than trying to buff immediately.

WIPE-ON FINISHES

Wipe-on finishes are especially popular with North American woodturners. They comprise a grain-filling polyurethane sealer that gives a clear, durable finish.

Applied with either a lint-free cloth or a high-quality brush, the drying time depends on the ambient temperature of the workshop, but your mill will usually be ready for additional coats within a few hours.

It is recommended that the turned item is lightly sanded with 400-grit sandpaper between coats. Three to four coats should be enough.

Wipe-on finishes are generally available in pint or 500 ml tins of satin, semi-gloss, or gloss.

BUFFING

All of my condiment holders receive the buffing process. I have three 6 in. (150 mm) loose-stitched mops, which I mount individually on a right-hand-threaded polishing mop adapter held in chuck jaws. An alternative is to purchase a Beall polishing system, which comes with everything you need to buff any wooden item.

The first mop is lightly loaded with tripoli powder, which is a gentle abrasive compound that will remove minor scratches. I should stress that this is not a substitute for a rushed sanding phase!

The second mop contains White Diamond, a micro-abrasive polishing compound, to remove traces of tripoli and create a deep shine. Do not press the condiment holder too hard, or "smearing" will appear on the polished surface.

The third and final mop is for applying carnauba wax. Apply a small amount and buff to create a final polish.

In addition, I have recently been applying by hand a wax developed for objects in the British Museum. The benefit of this Renaissance wax is that it does not show fingerprints. What you are trying to avoid is moist-handed chefs leaving permanent marks on your beautifully turned condiment holders!

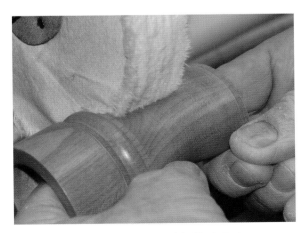

Buffing will keep your work looking its best

TURNED CONDIMENT HOLDERS: A BRIEF HISTORY

B y 2000 BC, people knew that adding salt to food stopped it going bad. Salt was, and still is, used to preserve meat, fish, and vegetables. The buying and selling of salt became one of the most important trading activities in the world.

Before considering possible designs for your salt and pepper containers, it is well worth taking a look at their history. The ancient Egyptians, Greeks, and Romans all used mortars and pestles for grinding, but the modern history of the subject begins in the 1500s.

SALT CONDIMENT HOLDERS

At the beginning of the 16th century, when Henry VIII was on the English throne, wealthy people would use a trencher (from Old French *tranchier*, "to cut") as a type of tableware. The trencher was originally a piece of stale bread,

Salt of the earth: salted cod hung up to cure naturally—still a common sight in fishing-based economies such as Newfoundland and Greenland

cut into a square shape and used as a plate. The trencher would soak up the juices of the meat that was served on it. At the end of the meal, the trencher could be eaten with the sauce, but it was more frequently given as alms to the poor, or thrown over the shoulder for the dogs to eat.

These square-cut trenchers of bread were gradually phased out during the 16th century. In their place, a square wooden bowl, with a circular hollow of about 6 in. (150 mm) in diameter, was used. In one corner of the square bowl there was often a second, smaller depression, which may have held the diner's personal supply of salt.

Salt was also placed in a container called a salt cellar or open salt, and would be offered to guests at the dining table. Salt cellars, made from solid silver, silver plate, or ceramics, continued to be popular until the mid-20th century.

You may come across other terms to describe containers for salt and other ingredients. I mention some below for your interest. You will see that they all lead to what we know today as a shaker.

A **cruet** with a pierced cover, used for dry ingredients such as salt, pepper, dry mustard, and sugar, may also be called a **caster** or **castor**. Some have a neck with interior threading for securing

This modern salt cellar is modeled on those of the 1840s

a threaded stopper, or external threading for a screw cap. Another name for these is **sifter**; today they are most likely to be called shakers.

A **condiment set** is a matched group of containers for pepper, salt, and mustard, usually with a tray or rack. It would be unusual to find a wooden condiment set; they are usually made from glass, silver, or ceramics.

A **cruet frame** or **cruet stand** was often part of a dinner service, to hold condiment containers such as cruets, mustard pots, casters (shakers), and muffineers (see following page).

Dredgers are also sometimes called muffineers—it does become confusing! They have a long history and are one of the oldest forms of kitchen utensils in existence. They are usually made from tin, and even today are used for sprinkling flour during baking or for holding a larger supply of salt or pepper.

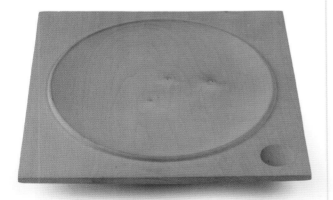

A modern reconstruction of a turned wooden trencher, with a large recess for food and a smaller recess for salt

A dredger for flour or other dry ingredients

Muffineers are usually made of silver, but wooden ones were also made; this one is in boxwood (see Project 9, pages 62–3)

A **muffineer** is another form of salt shaker. It's a container with holes in its threaded top to shake out sugar or salt. The top has a few holes around it to allow the salt to flow. It is perfectly acceptable to call a muffineer a shaker, since that's what it is. Are you as confused as I am by the different words used to describe similar things?

Substances like salt, sugar, and pepper were once extremely expensive, so storing them in a shaker protected them from dirt and moisture and reduced the risk of waste. Silver salt shakers dating back to the 16th century and even earlier are on display at museums with collections of culinary artifacts, and many of these shakers have very fine, beautiful designs from the hands of master craftsmen.

MODERN SALT SHAKERS

The first salt shakers in the modern sense of the term were invented in 1858 by the American, John Mason. These little screw-top jars were intended for keeping salt at the table and prevent it from caking because of humidity. From around 1870, salt was more finely milled, and ceramic containers with perforations in their tops were introduced.

By the early 20th century, moisture-absorbing agents such as magnesium carbonate were added to salt and it was sold as a finely ground powder. In 1924, iodized salt was developed for the table to help prevent the iodine deficiency and thyroid-gland problems common at the time. Around 1970, salt cellars were replaced with salt shakers as we know them today.

SALT GRINDERS

I have a French country-style salt grinder made from wood. The body is made from olivewood and the grinding mechanism itself is a wooden sphere with horizontal slots approximately $1/16$ in. (1.5 mm) wide. The sphere has a hole drilled through it for the turning peg and is secured with a nail. The grinding mechanism and the peg are made from boxwood. I am unable to put an accurate date on it—my guess is the first half of the 20th century. The salt crystals are inserted into the top to be ground, and the resulting ground crystals fall into the cup, which is then unscrewed to become the salt cellar.

A rustic French salt grinder in olivewood

Pepper Grinders

The trade in pepper predates the silk trade between East and West. In Roman times, pepper was as valuable as precious metals. In the Middle Ages, pepper was an accepted currency, and it was even used to pay taxes. Peppercorns were ideal for trade because they did not deteriorate over time, as long as they were kept dry and out of sunlight. The price of pepper eventually came down when it could be transported by ship and became an everyday item.

A pepper grinder was brought up from Henry VIII's battleship the *Mary Rose*, which sank in the Solent, just off Portsmouth on the south coast of England in 1545. She was on her way to engage the French in battle. It's thought that the ship fired a broadside at the enemy and was turning to fire the other broadside when water flooded into her open gunports and the ship suddenly capsized—in full view of Henry VIII, who was watching from the shore. I bet he was not amused! The original pepper grinder is preserved at the Mary Rose Museum in Portsmouth Historic Dockyard.

An early Tudor pepper grinder recovered from Henry VIII's flagship

In 1842, the French company Peugeot Frères developed the forerunner of the present-day pepper-grinder mechanism, using hardened steel. In 1997, they introduced a stainless-steel mechanism for salt. These products have a well-deserved reputation, but the mechanisms alone are not sold commercially. Mechanisms that are available to buy are detailed on pages 70–73.

Hardened plastic mechanisms like this one have been commercially available only in the last 20 years or so

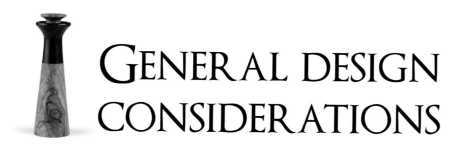

GENERAL DESIGN CONSIDERATIONS

There are a number of books available on the subject of design. Without going into the detail they provide, I'm just going to tell you how I go about designing a condiment holder. You may well want to take other people's ideas into consideration, too.

Some aspects of design are common to both shakers and mills. Here we will consider the first step:

Where do you get the idea for an original shape?

Shapes are everywhere: some of my projects were suggested by seashells, film characters, fruit, architecture, nature, ceramics, and bottles, to name just a few. There is nothing wrong in seeing a shape you like and tweaking it to add your personal touch—just don't plagiarize another person's work and pass it off as your own.

Let's assume that you have been sketching some ideas and you have settled on one you would like to progress. At this point you should ask yourself the following questions (more will need to be answered later):

Is the height of the shaker in proportion to its width?

Is it pleasing to your eye?

Is there a seamless flow between the curves and lines of the condiment container?

There will be times when you know that there is something wrong with your design, but you can't put your finger on what it is. This is a good time to ask someone else whose judgment you trust, whether they are fellow woodturners or friends and family. Of course, if the project is for yourself, then as long as you are happy with it, that is all that matters.

Your choice of wood is important. For example, a condiment holder turned in a plain, straight-grained wood may not be as eye-catching as it would be in a highly figured wood. Combinations of wood can provide an attractive contrast. Consider whether your design would benefit from any of the numerous texturing options, such as burning, coloring, chattering, or carving.

It's important to know which of the available accessories would best suit your design: these are described on pages 34–37 (for shakers) and 70–73 (for mills).

Even an everyday object like an onion bulb can provide inspiration.

The photographs on this page and opposite show a selection of everyday objects that might provide inspiration for a shaker or mill.
Can you see which of the projects and Gallery items they relate to?

SHAKERS

SHAKER ACCESSORIES

In less expensive restaurants, both in North America and in Europe, you are more likely to find a salt shaker on your table than a salt mill. Shakers found in restaurants are usually made from glass, stainless steel, or ceramics—but wooden shakers offer many exciting possibilities, as we shall see.

This section introduces the accessories available for making wooden salt and pepper shakers. It will help you choose accessories to suit your design.

Apart from the shape, there are two vital areas to be considered in your shaker design:

Getting the salt or pepper in

and, of course,

Getting the salt or pepper out.

GETTING THE SALT OR PEPPER IN

BUNGS
Most shakers are filled from the bottom and incorporate a bung, usually made from a rubber composition. A number of different sizes of bungs are available, ranging from ¾–1⁵⁄₁₆ in. (19–33 mm).

When you buy bungs it is unlikely that any drilling dimensions will be given. You may find it worthwhile drilling trial holes in a scrap piece of wood to check the fit. If possible, the bung hole should be surrounded by a shallow recess that provides an extra ³⁄₁₆ in. (5 mm) all around, to allow access with a fingernail or the end of a spoon to remove the bung. This shallow hole should be drilled before the actual bung hole.

INCORPORATING SCREW THREADS
If you wish, you could incorporate a wooden screw at the bottom of your shaker. However, this does raise the problem of the salt getting between the threads and causing wear and tear, or tightness when unscrewing the thread.

Woodturned threads can be designed to be undone by gripping either a turned button, a plug, or the top half of the shaker body. Examples of threaded shakers are the Bell shaker on pages 54–57 and the Muffineer on pages 62–63.

PLUGS AND O-RINGS
It is important that the plug in the top of the shaker fits well—the last thing you want is for it to fall out when shaking out salt or pepper.

A turned wooden plug can be fitted with a rubber or plastic O-ring, obtained from a plumbing or hardware store, to provide a reliable seal. The O-ring is retained by a groove cut in the plug, and you may need to adapt the depth of

Rubber bungs

A screw-top shaker with only two holes in the top to control the flow of salt

the groove to get a good fit with the O-rings you have. I would recommend that you turn a dummy plug in an inexpensive wood to obtain the right dimensions for your O-ring before turning the real thing.

TAPERED PLUGS

I tend to use these for combo mills. The plug is basically a tapered piece of hardwood. An example can be seen on page 151.

HINT:
It is a good idea to buy at least twice as many O-rings as you need. They can get damaged when you take them off repeatedly during the turning and fitting phase.

A turned plug fitted with an O-ring

GETTING THE SALT OR PEPPER OUT

SALT AND PEPPER CAPS

Salt and pepper caps are commercially available in chrome; sizes range from $^{13}/_{16}$ in. (21 mm) to $1^{3}/_{8}$ in. (35 mm). Some have three pointed legs that hold the cap in the wood; these are glued or gently knocked into the top of the shaker. You should consider drilling $^{1}/_{16}$ in. (1.5 mm) pilot holes for the legs, as there is a possibility of the wood splitting without them.

DRILLED HOLES

If you prefer not to use commercial accessories, there are two options:

1 Drill directly into the top of the shaker using either a small handheld power drill or a drill press.

2 Turn an insert of contrasting wood, which can then be shaped to match the top of the shaker.

Option 1
This is probably the least time-consuming option, but your marking and drilling must be accurate for the shaker to look right.

Two examples of chrome caps. The one on the right has prongs to embed in the wood

A turned insert with a single drilled hole for salt

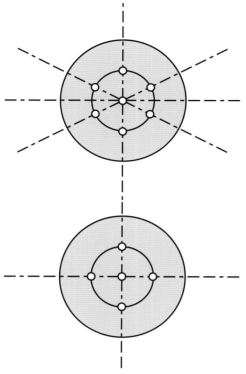

Some suggested arrangements of holes for a pepper shaker. Holes are 1/16 in. (1.5 mm) diameter

The identification of salt or pepper depends on the number of holes. Usually there are between three and seven holes for pepper and one or two for salt. The size of the drilled hole will depend on your views of the user's requirements. Usually a 3/32 in. (2 mm) hole will suffice, but I suggest that if you are making a shaker for the first time you might want to start with a smaller hole.

Option 2

For this option, the hole that forms the salt or pepper reservoir is drilled all the way through and an insert is made to fit the opening at the top. Use the long point of a skew chisel to form a small step in the top of the shaker before gluing it in. Light and dark woods can be used to differentiate the salt and the pepper shakers. Some of the woods you could use for the salt are pau amarello, box, sycamore, or maple; for the pepper, ebony, blackwood, or rosewood. Naturally your choice will depend on the wood you have used for the shakers.

The wood for the insert is rough-turned and faced off. Turn a tenon that can be held in compression jaws. Then, holding the wood by the tenon, turn the insert to a size close to the required diameter and offer the top of the shaker to it to check for size. Keep removing wood until you have a snug fit, then part off approximately 1/4 in. (6 mm) in length. You now have two possibilities for drilling your insert:

1 Glue the turned insert into the shaker, then drill the holes as for option 1 above. As before, the marking and drilling must be accurate for the shaker to look right.

2 Turn two hardwood jigs as shown in the illustrations, using a tight-grained hardwood such as ebony or box. Reduce the diameter of the insert to allow it to sit in the 19/32 in. (15 mm) hole in jig no.1 (see photo 2, page 44). Part off the

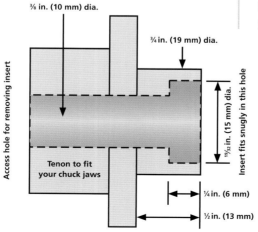

Jig no. 1 for holding the insert while drilling a single salt insert on the lathe or a pepper insert on the bench

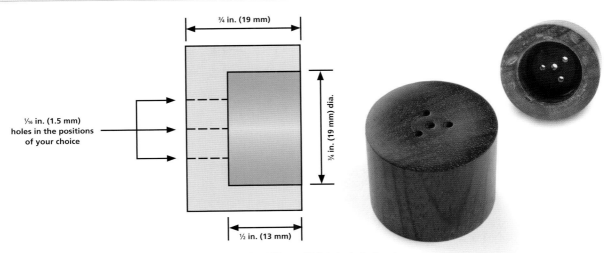

¾ in. (19 mm)

¹⁄₁₆ in. (1.5 mm)
holes in the positions
of your choice

¾ in. (19 mm) dia.

½ in. (13 mm)

Jig no. 2 for drilling multiple holes in the insert

insert to approximately ¼ in. (6 mm) in length. The insert piece can now be placed in the ¹⁹⁄₃₂ in. (15 mm) hole of jig no. 1, and jig no. 2 placed over it (see photo 3, page 44). Now drill through the pre-drilled holes in jig no. 2. The ⅜ in. (10 mm) hole through jig no. 1 provides access for knocking the insert out if it is a tight fit.

To make a single salt hole, jig no. 1 can be held by its tenon, the insert secured in the ¹⁹⁄₃₂ in. (15 mm) hole and drilled on the lathe; jig no. 2 is not required.

Glue the insert into the top of the shaker using cyanoacrylate (Super Glue), then complete the turning and sand the top of the shaker as needed.

This is a more time-consuming method, but if you are turning a number of shakers it ensures that the holes are accurately drilled.

GETTING THE SALT OR PEPPER BOTH IN AND OUT

SHAKERS WITH SCREW CAP
Commercially available screw containers can be incorporated into a designed wooden shaker. Project 2 (pages 46–47) shows an example of a shaker using a container.

The containers shown are 2 in. (50 mm) in length and just less than 1 in. (25 mm) in diameter at the top, tapering down to ⅞ in. (22 mm) at the base. The container can be glued in using silicone, which will allow for any movement in the wood.

FINALLY...

How about putting the salt or pepper in at the same place you get it out? Sounds crazy, doesn't it? The shaker in question will probably never be found in a restaurant but you might like to make one to confuse your dinner guests. You'll find my Upside-Down shaker in Project 10 (pages 64–65).

These ready-made screw-top containers can be incorporated in a turned shaker

FINALIZING A SHAKER DESIGN

Before starting to make your shakers, a little extra preparation can save a lot of problems later on. Set out your design to scale, including the holes and the dimensions required for your chosen accessories. This will reduce the "designer firewood" pile.

Turn a prototype shaker between centers, using softwood or scrap hardwood. It is not usually necessary to drill any holes at this stage.

The prototype shaker can now be placed at eye level some 6 ft. (2 m) away and looked at to see if it is in balance. You may decide that it is not wide enough, the curves are the wrong depth, or the waistline is not narrow enough—there could be any number of changes that might improve the overall look and balance of the shaker and help it meet the design criteria described on page 30.

If you are reasonably happy with it, spray the prototype shaker matte black, stand it at the same distance as before, and ask the question, "Does it still meet my design criteria?" In the example shown opposite, I went one stage further and fitted a metal cap. "Does that size of pepper cap look right?" is what I was asking myself. The matte-black paint draws your eye to the shape, so you are not distracted by any markings or grain in the wood.

There have been many occasions when it wasn't until this stage that I saw something was wrong. I often request a second opinion from a fellow woodturner or a family member just in case I am being hard on myself. If changes are needed, it is not a problem—subject, that is, to there being a need to remove wood rather than add it! If necessary, make a note of any dimension changes, then add the piece to the "designer firewood" pile and start again.

The next decision to be made is which wood would best show off this design. Unless the client has asked for a particular wood, it is worth looking carefully at the design with regard to the suitability of the woods available to you. Given that shakers are mostly made in pairs, they are best made from the same length of wood to ensure similar grain direction and color.

When you are happy with the look of the shaker, double-check all the dimensions and update your diagram accordingly. At this point you should make a simple diagram of the blank required, giving overall dimensions and allowing extra for waste and for any tenons or dovetails needed during the turning process.

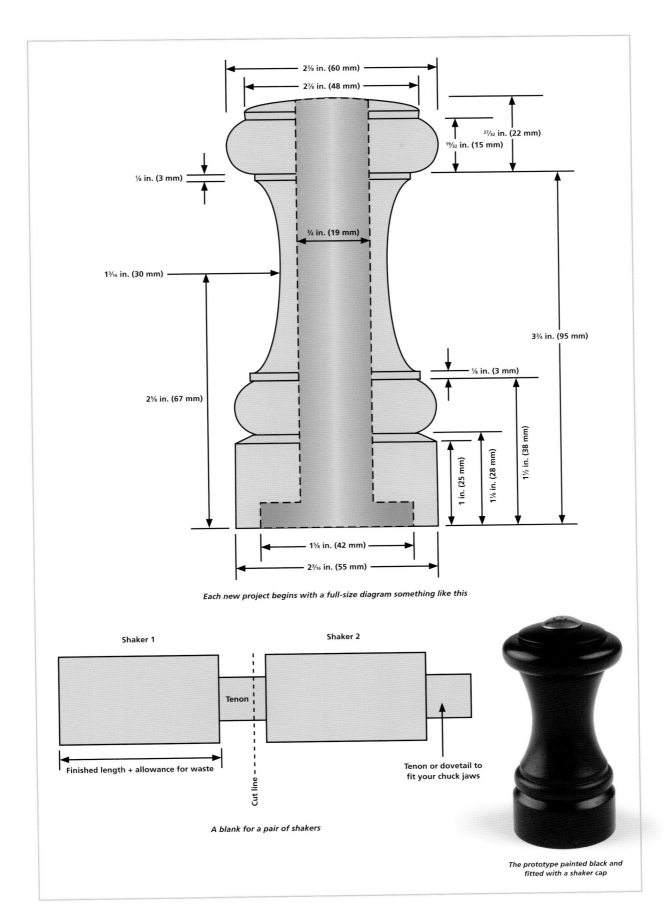

2³⁄₈ in. (60 mm)

2⁷⁄₈ in. (48 mm)

²⁷⁄₃₂ in. (22 mm)

¹⁹⁄₃₂ in. (15 mm)

⅛ in. (3 mm)

¾ in. (19 mm)

1³⁄₁₆ in. (30 mm)

3¾ in. (95 mm)

⅛ in. (3 mm)

2⅝ in. (67 mm)

1 in. (25 mm)

1⅛ in. (28 mm)

1½ in. (38 mm)

1⅝ in. (42 mm)

2³⁄₁₆ in. (55 mm)

Each new project begins with a full-size diagram something like this

Shaker 1

Shaker 2

Tenon

Cut line

Finished length + allowance for waste

Tenon or dovetail to
fit your chuck jaws

A blank for a pair of shakers

*The prototype painted black and
fitted with a shaker cap*

SHAKER PROJECTS

1 GARLIC

■ Level of difficulty: **Beginner**

TOOLS

¾ in. (19 mm) spindle roughing gouge
½ in. (13 mm) spindle gouge
½ in. (13 mm) beading and parting tool
½ in. (13 mm) skew chisel
⅛ in. (3 mm) parting tool
1/16 in. (1.5 mm) twist drill
Jigs for drilling inserts (see pages 36–37)

Accessories required:
Bung

WOOD

English ash for shaker body; pau amarello and ebony for inserts

Height: 2⅞ in. (73 mm)
Diameter: 2⅞ in. (73 mm)
Blank dimensions:
Shaker body: 3 x 3 x 6⅛ in. (75 x 75 x 155 mm)
Inserts: Each 1 x 1 x 2 in. (25 x 25 x 50 mm)
These dimensions allow sufficient wood for both pieces, including facing off and tenons or dovetails that will be removed as the project proceeds.

While mills are often made as single items, shakers tend to be made as pairs. If you plan to use the same wood for both, it is best to make up a blank from a single piece of wood, as shown on page 39, to provide a continuous flow of the grain.

The Garlic shaker is based on an elephant-garlic bulb given to me by a friend.

This project introduces both the drilling process and the use of inserts of contrasting wood to differentiate the two shakers.

English ash was the nearest I could get to the color and grain markings found in a garlic bulb; American ash would also be suitable. For the contrasting inserts I chose pau amarello and ebony. A 1 in. (25 mm) rubber bung at the base will hold the salt or pepper in, and at the top of the shaker an insert of contrasting wood will be turned and drilled with 1/16 in. (1.5 mm) holes to let the contents out.

If you require more detailed information on methods of holding the blanks, sanding, and sealing the wood, refer to pages 22–25 and 82–83.

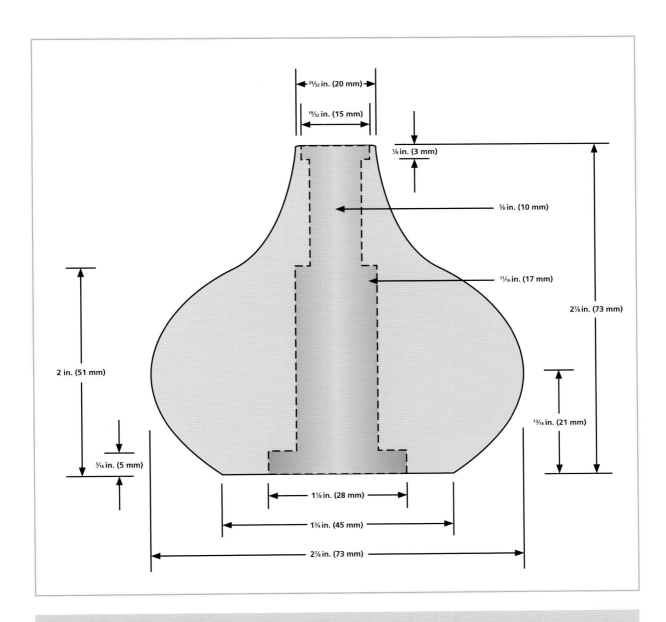

25/32 in. (20 mm)

19/32 in. (15 mm)

1/8 in. (3 mm)

3/8 in. (10 mm)

11/16 in. (17 mm)

2 in. (51 mm)

2⅞ in. (73 mm)

13/16 in. (21 mm)

3/16 in. (5 mm)

1⅛ in. (28 mm)

1¾ in. (45 mm)

2⅞ in. (73 mm)

INSERT JIGS:

A pair of jigs as shown on pages 36–37 will allow accurate turning and drilling of the inserts for the top of the shaker. I recommend making the jigs first, so you won't have to remove the shaker from the lathe halfway through the turning process. The diagram on the right shows the positions of the pepper holes to be drilled in jig no. 2 for this project.

Alternatively, you can do without the jigs by turning and drilling the insert first and then offering it to the shaker as you open the ⅜ in. (10 mm) hole. You will have to rely on measuring the holes for the pepper accurately, then holding the insert with your fingers while drilling the holes. If you are likely to make more than one pair of Garlic shakers, then the jigs are well worth making. The choice is yours.

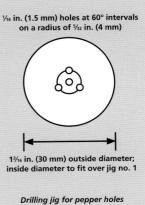

1/16 in. (1.5 mm) holes at 60° intervals on a radius of 5/32 in. (4 mm)

1³/16 in. (30 mm) outside diameter; inside diameter to fit over jig no. 1

Drilling jig for pepper holes

TURNING THE INSERTS

1 Start with a 1 x 1 x 2 in. (25 x 25 x 50 mm) section of your chosen wood, held in compression jaws or between centers. Turn a tenon to fit your preferred lathe jaws. Turn the body of the piece to a size just over the required diameter of ¹⁹⁄₃₂ in. (15 mm).

2 Do a trial fit (jig no. 1, see page 36) to check the insert for size. Keep removing wood until you have a snug fit, then part off the insert to approximately ¼ in. (6 mm) in length. Then repeat for the other insert.

3 Place the insert piece in the sizing jig (jig no. 1) and cover it with the drilling jig (jig no. 2). The appropriate holes can now be drilled on a drill press.

TURNING THE SHAKER

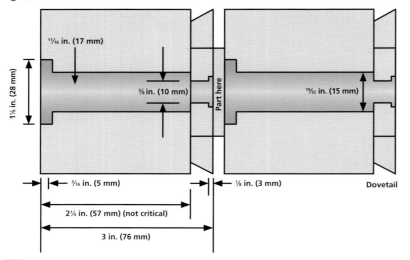

¹¹⁄₁₆ in. (17 mm)

1⅛ in. (28 mm)

⅜ in. (10 mm)

Part here

¹⁹⁄₃₂ in. (15 mm)

³⁄₁₆ in. (5 mm)

⅛ in. (3 mm)

Dovetail

2¼ in. (57 mm) (not critical)

3 in. (76 mm)

4 Rough out the blank as shown, saw or part in two, then mount one of the blanks in either compression or dovetail jaws. The dovetail tenon is larger than the neck of the shaker but fits within the overall dimensions of the shaker.

5 Face off the bottom and drill the two holes for the bung and the main part of the reservoir. If necessary, you can use a skew chisel to adjust the drilled hole sizes so they fit the bungs you have. Sand to 400 grit. If you are planning to use sealer, this can be applied to the bottom now. Remove the blank from the lathe.

6 Using any suitable hardwood, turn a plug that will be a jam fit in the reservoir and bung holes previously drilled. Mount the blank on this and, with the help of the tailstock, ensure that it is running true. Mark 2⅞ in. (73 mm) from the base of the shaker and face off to this length.

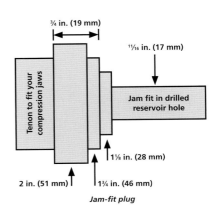

¾ in. (19 mm)

1¹⁄₁₆ in. (17 mm)

Tenon to fit your compression jaws

Jam fit in drilled reservoir hole

1⅛ in. (28 mm)

2 in. (51 mm)

1¾ in. (46 mm)

Jam-fit plug

7 Remove the tailstock support temporarily while you drill the ⅜ in. (10 mm) hole from the top of the shaker to meet the ¹¹⁄₁₆ in. (17 mm) hole previously drilled.

8 Bring the tailstock back up to support the shaker. Use a ⅜ in. (10 mm) or ½ in. (13 mm) spindle gouge to shape most of the outside, leaving the very top for now. When you are happy with the outside shape, sand to 400 grit and seal.

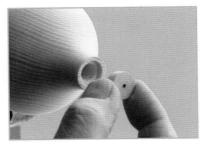

9 Now is the time to make room for the ¹⁹⁄₃₂ in. (15 mm) insert. Given that the top of the shaker is supported some 3½ in. (95 mm) from the holding chuck and is quite narrow at the tailstock end, it is advisable to remove the jam chuck and mount the bottom of the shaker in expansion jaws instead. Make sure that the shaker is running true, then open the ⅜ in. (10 mm) hole to the width of the insert and ⅛ in. (3 mm) deep, using the long point of a ½ in. (13 mm) skew. Glue the insert into the top of the shaker using cyanoacrylate (Super Glue).

10 When the glue is set, you can turn the very top of the shaker to a dome shape. Take light cuts with a ¼ in. (6 mm) or ⅜ in. (10 mm) spindle gouge. When you are happy with the shape of the top, sand down to 400 grit.

Finishing

A choice of finishing methods is described on pages 22–25. For this pair of ash shakers, I used a 50% mix of melamine lacquer and cellulose thinners, applied with a brush with the lathe turned off. They were sprayed with an acrylic lacquer, and, after 24 hours, buffed using first White Diamond and then carnauba wax.

2 DOG BONE

■ Level of difficulty: **Beginner**

TOOLS

¾ in. (19mm) spindle roughing gouge
⅜ in. (10mm) spindle gouge
½ in. (13mm) spindle gouge
½ in. (13mm) beading and parting tool
½ in. (13mm) skew chisel
⅛ in. (3mm) parting tool

Accessories required:
Salt container (for yew shaker)
Salt cap and bung (for laburnum shaker)

WOOD

Yew and laburnum

Height: 3¾ in. (95 mm)
Diameter: 2¾ in. (70 mm)
Blank dimensions: 3 x 3 x 4½ in.
(76 x 76 x 115 mm) for each shaker.
This allows for holding tenons.

T his very simple shape lends itself to incorporating a number of the available shaker accessories. Two possible approaches are described below.

The diagram opposite gives the dimensions of the basic shaker and shows the holes that need to be drilled for both the salt container and the cap accessories. Both blanks need to allow for a tenon to hold the shaker when drilling the necessary holes.

The yew shaker holds a ready-made salt container (illustrated on page 37). Holding the blank by the tenon at its base, drill a hole to fit your container snugly; mine was 1 in. (25 mm)

Laburnum shaker with salt cap and bung

Yew shaker incorporating a ready-made salt container

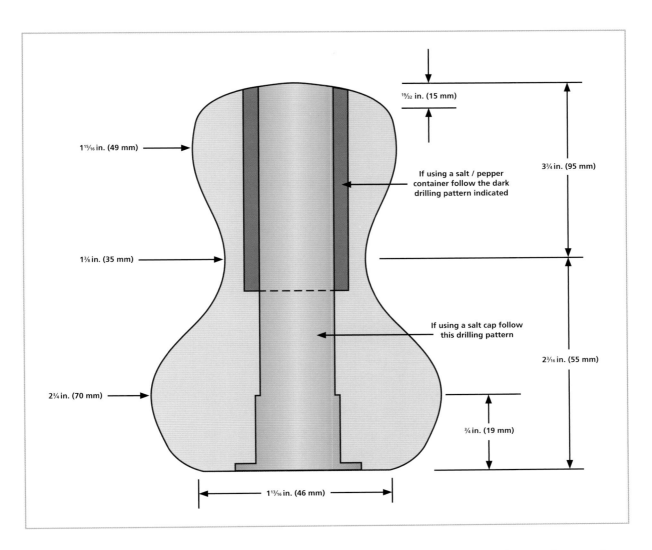

1¹⁵⁄₁₆ in. (49 mm)

1⅜ in. (35 mm)

2¾ in. (70 mm)

1¹³⁄₁₆ in. (46 mm)

¹⁹⁄₃₂ in. (15 mm)

If using a salt / pepper container follow the dark drilling pattern indicated

3¾ in. (95 mm)

If using a salt cap follow this drilling pattern

2³⁄₁₆ in. (55 mm)

¾ in. (19 mm)

diameter by 2 in. (51 mm) deep. I then made a 1 in. (25 mm) jam chuck for the shaker to slip onto while the outside was shaped. Turn away the tenon at the base of the shaker and turn the base slightly concave before finishing. The container is glued in place using silicone. This shaker is finished with acrylic lacquer, buffed, and waxed.

The laburnum shaker uses a salt cap and a bung. This time the holding tenon is turned at the top to allow for the drilling of the two holes required for the bung and the lower part of the reservoir. Following this, the base of the shaker is held in expansion jaws where the bung fits. The holding tenon is removed and the hole for the salt cap is drilled to meet the previously drilled holes. The tailstock is brought up and the outside shaped.

This shaker was finished with several coats of finishing oil before buffing and waxing. The salt cap was fitted using cyanoacrylate (Super Glue).

▶ OTHER OPTIONS

Using a bung at the base, two additional options are:

1 Working from the base, drill the salt reservoir hole to within ⁵⁄₃₂ in. (4 mm) of the top, then drill holes in the top for either salt or pepper.

2 Drill the reservoir hole all the way through and form a step in the top before gluing in pre-drilled, contrasting wood inserts for the salt and pepper, as for Project 1.

3 BEEHIVE

■ Level of difficulty: **Beginner**

TOOLS
¾ in. (19 mm) spindle roughing gouge
⅜ in. (10 mm) spindle gouge
½ in. (13 mm) spindle gouge
½ in. (13 mm) beading and parting tool
⅛ in. (3 mm) parting tool
³⁄₁₆ in. (5 mm) fluted parting tool

Accessories required: Bung

WOOD
American cherry; bloodwood for the contrasting insert

Height: 3¹⁄₃₂ in. (77 mm)
Diameter: 2⅝ in. (67 mm)
Blank dimensions:
Body: 2⅞ x 2⅞ x 4½ in. (73 x 73 x 115 mm)
Insert: 2⅞ x 2⅞ x 1⁵⁄₁₆ in. (73 x 73 x 30 mm)
These dimensions allow for facing off and turning either a tenon or a dovetail that will be removed as the project proceeds.

The design of this shaker recalls the traditional "skep" beehive made from plaited straw rope—once a familiar sight in rural areas but now quite a rarity.

The Beehive shaker uses a bung at its base and drilled holes at the top. The top can be the same wood as the body, or a contrasting wood to differentiate the salt and pepper.

Rough-turn the body and insert the blank between centers (see diagram, bottom page 49).

To make the body, the tenon or dovetail at the top of the blank is held in compression jaws. Ensure it is running true, then face off the base and drill the two holes for the bung. You may find it easier to start turning the lower half of the body at this time—when the body has been reversed, the chuck jaws may restrict access to the very bottom of the body.

The body is reversed and held using expansion jaws in the larger of the two bung holes. When running true, and with the tailstock giving support, remove the tenon or dovetail and drill a 1 in. (25 mm) hole to a depth of 2 in. (51 mm).

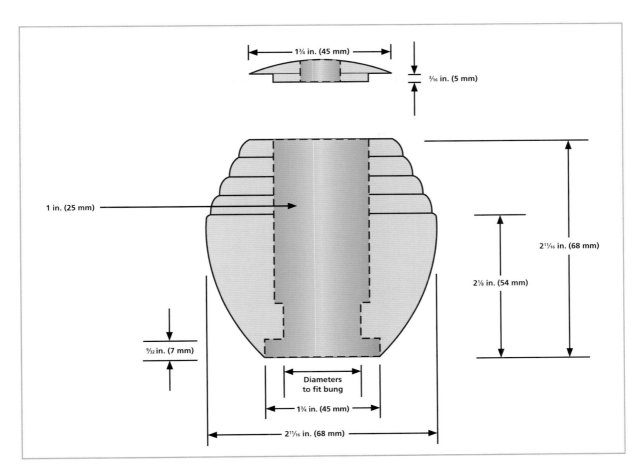

1¾ in. (45 mm)

³⁄₁₆ in. (5 mm)

1 in. (25 mm)

2¹¹⁄₁₆ in. (68 mm)

2⅛ in. (54 mm)

⁹⁄₃₂ in. (7 mm)

Diameters to fit bung

1¾ in. (45 mm)

2¹¹⁄₁₆ in. (68 mm)

The tailstock is used to support the body while the rest of the outside is shaped and the beads added using a ³⁄₁₆ in. (5 mm) fluted parting tool.

Next, turn the insert. The insert blank is mounted by its tenon in compression jaws and the tenon reduced to a snug fit in the body's 1 in. (25 mm) reservoir. This is a good time to drill the necessary salt or pepper holes, off the lathe.

The body of the shaker is once again held at its base in expansion jaws while the top insert is glued into the body, supported by the tailstock until dry. The top of the shaker can now be shaped to flow into the body. After sanding and sealing, the shaker is ready for your chosen finish.

Salt shaker in American cherry

Pepper shaker with bloodwood insert

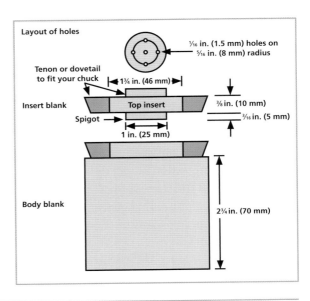

Layout of holes

¹⁄₁₆ in. (1.5 mm) holes on ⁵⁄₁₆ in. (8 mm) radius

Tenon or dovetail to fit your chuck

1¾ in. (46 mm)

Insert blank

Top insert

⅜ in. (10 mm)

³⁄₁₆ in. (5 mm)

Spigot

1 in. (25 mm)

Body blank

2¾ in. (70 mm)

4 OFFSET

■ Level of difficulty: **Intermediate**

TOOLS

¾ in. (19 mm) spindle roughing gouge
⅜ in. (10 mm) spindle gouge
½ in. (13 mm) spindle gouge
½ in. (13 mm) beading and parting tool
½ in. (13 mm) skew chisel
⅛ in. (3 mm) parting tool
¹⁄₁₆ in. (1.5 mm) twist drill

Accessories required: Bung

WOOD

Mulberry branch wood; pau amarello and ebony for the inserts

Height: 4–4¼ in. (102–108 mm)
Diameter: 2–2¼ in. (51–57 mm)
Blank dimensions:
Shaker: 2–2¼ x 2–2¼ x 5 in.
(51–57 x 51–57 x 127 mm)
Inserts: Contrasting wood, ¹³⁄₁₆ x ¹³⁄₁₆ x 2 in.
(21 x 21 x 51 mm)
These dimensions include sufficient wood for facing off and for a tenon or dovetail that will be removed as the project progresses.

This shaker uses a piece of branch wood with interesting bark. Two-thirds of the bark will be turned away to reveal the grain. Look for a piece that does not have a knot in the area where the bark will remain.

HOLLOWING THE SHAKER

Between centers, turn a tenon or dovetail on the end where the bark will be removed. Holding the blank in compression mode, drill the holes for the bung and the start of the reservoir hole, to a depth of 2 in. (51 mm). Reverse, holding the base of the shaker in expansion mode, and part off to the desired length.

MAKING THE JAM CHUCK

The blank for the jam chuck measures 2 x 2 x 3⅝ in. (51 x 51 x 92 mm). Mark position 1 at each end of the blank, and position 2 at the tailstock end, ⁵⁄₁₆ in. (8 mm) away from position 1. Mount the blank between centers, using position 1 at each end, and begin turning the jam chuck as shown. (A Steb drive would be useful here.)

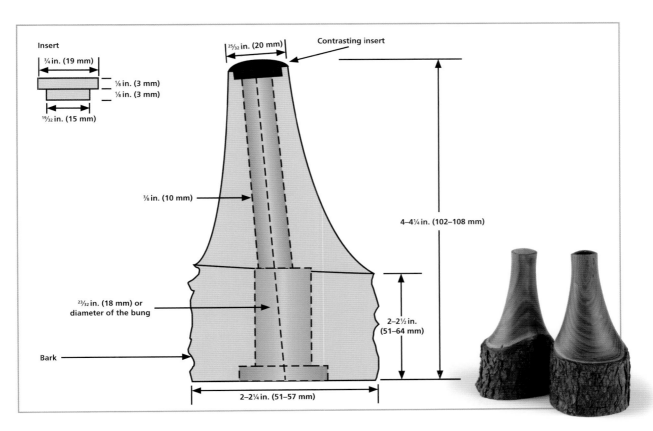

Insert

¾ in. (19 mm)

⅛ in. (3 mm)
⅛ in. (3 mm)

¹⁹⁄₃₂ in. (15 mm)

²⁵⁄₃₂ in. (20 mm)

Contrasting insert

⅜ in. (10 mm)

4–4¼ in. (102–108 mm)

²³⁄₃₂ in. (18 mm) or
diameter of the bung

2–2½ in.
(51–64 mm)

Bark

2–2¼ in. (51–57 mm)

Turn the shaft to fit the reservoir as accurately as possible. Now reposition the blank so the tailstock engages position 2, and turn piece A to fit your compression jaws. Finally, cut off piece B.

TURNING THE SHAKER

Mount the jig in compression jaws and place the shaker blank over it with the tailstock supporting it. If the shaft is too loose in the reservoir hole, wrap a piece of masking tape around it. Before turning the outside, reinforce the part of the bark that will remain with a thin coating of cyanoacrylate (Super Glue).

Rough-turn the concave shape before drilling the ⅜ in. (10 mm) hole to meet the reservoir hole already drilled. Open the top to a diameter of ¹⁹⁄₃₂ in. (15 mm) and a depth of ⅛ in. (3 mm) to receive the insert, which will be glued in later.

MAKING THE INSERTS

The inserts are turned and drilled as shown in Project 1 (see pages 42–45).

COMPLETING THE SHAKER

Remount the jam chuck and shaker, ensuring it is running true. With tailstock support, complete the turning of the outside of the shaker. Sand and seal. Glue the insert with cyanoacrylate and, when dry, turn a dome. Finish as desired.

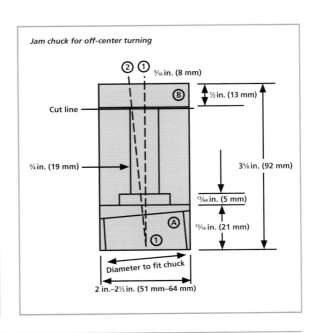

Jam chuck for off-center turning

⁵⁄₁₆ in. (8 mm)

⑧

½ in. (13 mm)

Cut line

¾ in. (19 mm)

3⅝ in. (92 mm)

¹³⁄₆₄ in. (5 mm)

¹³⁄₁₆ in. (21 mm)

Ⓐ

Diameter to fit chuck

2 in.–2½ in. (51 mm–64 mm)

5 DONUT

Level of difficulty: **Intermediate**

TOOLS
¾ in. (19 mm) spindle roughing gouge
⅜ in. (10 mm) spindle gouge
⅛ in. (3 mm) parting tool

Accessories required: Bung

WOOD
Walnut and pau amarello

Height: 2²¹⁄₃₂ in. (68 mm)
Diameter: 2²⁹⁄₃₂ in. (74 mm)
Blank dimensions:
Outer sections: Each 3⅛ x 1⅛ x 3⁹⁄₁₆ in. (79 x 28 x
90 mm).* At least one side should be planed.
Inner section: 3⅛ x ¼ x 3⁹⁄₁₆ in. (79 x 6 x
90 mm).* The blank should be planed down to
a uniform ¼ in. (6 mm) thickness.
Inserts: Contrasting woods, each 1⅛ x 1⅛ x
2¼ in. (28.5 x 28.5 x 57 mm)
The dimensions given allow for the tenon at
the top.

**It is advisable to double these lengths to enable both
shakers to be prepared from the same plank of wood.*

This shaker is made up of three pieces of wood, which are laminated together and then turned into a circular form.

Glue and clamp the three pieces of wood required for the pair of shakers. Once dry, bandsaw in two. Mark up and drill a 1 in. (25 mm) diameter hole to a depth of 1 in. (25 mm) in the center of the blank to receive the insert. At what will be the base and top of the shaker, mark the centers and turn a tenon. Remove from the lathe.

Hold the blank by its tenon, supported by the tailstock, and remove ¼ in. (6 mm) to form the flat base before drilling the holes for the bung and the reservoir. Sand and seal. Take care not to go too deep with the hole for the reservoir. Remove from the lathe and cut off the tenon.

Mount the blank in expansion jaws by means of the 1 in. (25 mm) hole drilled earlier. Turn the outside diameter to 2¹⁵⁄₁₆ in. (74.5 mm). Drill the second button hole through to meet the existing one, then remove from the lathe.

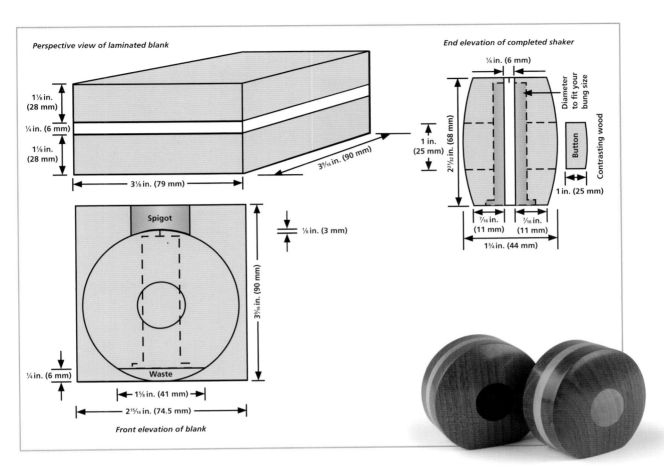

Perspective view of laminated blank

1⅛ in. (28 mm)

¼ in. (6 mm)

1⅛ in. (28 mm)

3⅛ in. (79 mm)

3⁹⁄₁₆ in. (90 mm)

End elevation of completed shaker

¼ in. (6 mm)

Diameter to fit your bung size

1 in. (25 mm)

2²¹⁄₃₂ in. (68 mm)

Button

Contrasting wood

1 in. (25 mm)

⁷⁄₁₆ in. (11 mm)

⁷⁄₁₆ in. (11 mm)

1¾ in. (44 mm)

Spigot

⅛ in. (3 mm)

3⁹⁄₁₆ in. (90 mm)

¼ in. (6 mm)

Waste

1⅝ in. (41 mm)

2¹⁵⁄₁₆ in. (74.5 mm)

Front elevation of blank

Turn a cylinder from one of the contrasting woods, 1 in. (25 mm) diameter, 1¾ in. (44 mm) long, for the two buttons. Keep offering the blank to the cylinder to obtain a snug fit. Allow enough length for it to pass through the shaker body and touch the expansion jaws. Part off or bandsaw the button.

With the blank remounted in the expansion jaws, push in the button cylinder until it meets the jaws. Begin to shape the convex curve as shown in the end elevation diagram. There should be enough of the button protruding to allow you to finish turning the convex curve.

Through the bung hole, mark the end of the button cylinder you have just turned. Remove the shaker from the chuck jaws and poke the button out. Cut the cylinder at the point just marked. This allows the reservoir to be clear of the button. This will be button no. 1. Do not glue it in yet.

Cut button no. 2 to the same length as button no.1. Pay attention to the button's grain direction and use a few drops of cyanoacrylate (Super Glue) to glue button 2 in place.

Reverse the shaker blank on the expansion jaws and repeat the outside shaping as before. Sand and seal.

Carefully push button 1 into place, aligning its grain with that of button 2, with a few drops of cyanoacrylate to hold it. If necessary, sand button 1 by hand to ensure a smooth, convex finish. Seal and finish as required, then buff using a micro-abrasive polishing compound and carnauba wax.

Finally, drill the exit hole(s) for the salt and pepper using a ¹⁄₁₆ in. (1.5 mm) twist drill.

6 BELL (VERSION 1)

Level of difficulty: **Beginner**

TOOLS
¾ in. (19 mm) spindle roughing gouge
⅜ in. (10 mm) spindle gouge
¼ in. (6 mm) spindle gouge
½ in. (13 mm) beading and parting tool
½ in. (13 mm) skew chisel
1/16 in. (1.5 mm) parting tool
⅛ in. (3 mm) parting tool
⅛ in. (3 mm) round-nosed scraper (see text)

Accessories required: Bung

WOOD
Beli

Height: 2 9/16 in. (65 mm)
Diameter: 2⅞ in. (72 mm)
Blank dimensions: 2¾ x 2¾ x 4 in.
(70 x 70 x 101 mm)
These dimensions allow for facing off and
for tenons or dovetails that will be removed
as the project proceeds.

The Bell shaker is based on some bells I saw in the English Lake District. American readers may be reminded of a famous national symbol.

Two versions of the shaker are described. The first uses a bung in its base to hold in the salt or pepper. In the second, the top half of the shaker unscrews to allow it to be filled.

USING A BUNG
The wood chosen for version 1 is beli. This is similar in color to zebrano, but denser and nicer to work. Rough out the blank between centers (see diagram, bottom page 55). Remount the blank in the compression jaws, face off the bottom, drill

the two recesses for the bung as shown in the main diagram, and sand. If necessary, adjust the recess sizes to fit the bung you have. Turn the bottom bead.

Remove the blank from the chuck, then point-mark and drill (preferably using a drill press) the 1/16 in. (1.5 mm) holes, as appropriate, ¾ in. (19 mm) deep through the tenon. Part the top and base, using either a bandsaw or, after remounting, a parting tool.

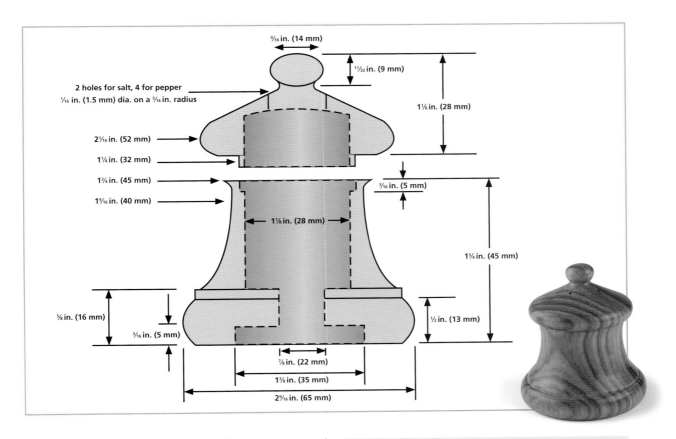

9/16 in. (14 mm)

2 holes for salt, 4 for pepper
1/16 in. (1.5 mm) dia. on a 5/16 in. radius

11/32 in. (9 mm)

1 1/8 in. (28 mm)

2 1/16 in. (52 mm)

1 1/4 in. (32 mm)

1 3/4 in. (45 mm)

1 9/16 in. (40 mm)

3/16 in. (5 mm)

1 1/8 in. (28 mm)

1 3/4 in. (45 mm)

5/8 in. (16 mm)

3/16 in. (5 mm)

1/2 in. (13 mm)

7/8 in. (22 mm)

1 3/8 in. (35 mm)

2 9/16 in. (65 mm)

Mount the base using either a jam chuck or expansion jaws in the bung recess. Ensure that it is running true, then face off to the correct length and drill the two holes for the rebate and body cavity, as shown in the diagram above. Complete the outside turning and sanding of the main body.

Remount the top of the shaker on its tenon. Turn the spigot to a diameter that ensures a snug fit into the base. Drill the 1 1/8 in. (28 mm) hole accurately to 1/2 in. (13 mm) depth. Dome the top of this recess—a 1/4 in. (6 mm) spindle gouge and a 1/2 in. (13 mm) round-nosed scraper will do the job—and you should see the holes you drilled earlier.

Remove the top from the chuck and remount the base. Line up the grain between the two parts and glue them together, bringing up the tailstock to clamp them firmly.

When dry, complete the turning of the Bell. To help turn the underside curve on the knob at the top of the bell, consider fashioning a 1/8 in. (3 mm) round-headed scraper from an old wood chisel.

▶ **HINT:**
If you are unable to drill the 1/16 in. (1.5 mm) holes using a drill press, use a handheld drill set to high speed.

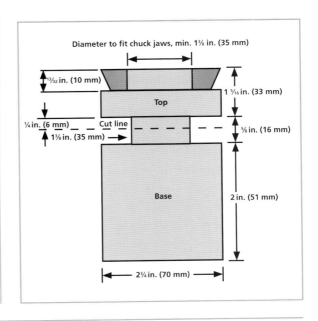

Diameter to fit chuck jaws, min. 1 3/8 in. (35 mm)

13/32 in. (10 mm)

1 5/16 in. (33 mm)

Top

1/4 in. (6 mm)

Cut line

5/8 in. (16 mm)

1 3/8 in. (35 mm)

Base

2 in. (51 mm)

2 3/4 in. (70 mm)

BELL (VERSION 2)

TOOLS

Same as for version 1 (pages 54–55), plus:
½ in. (13 mm) round-nosed scraper
Recess tool and armrest support
20 tpi thread chasers

Accessories required: None

WOOD

Indian rosewood

Height: 2⁹⁄₁₆ in. (65 mm)
Diameter: 2⅞ in. (72 mm)
Blank dimensions: 2¾ x 2¾ x 4 in.
(70 x 70 x 101 mm)

Indian rosewood was chosen for this version, as it is a harder wood than beli and more suitable for thread-chasing.

Begin by roughing out the blank and sawing it into two (see diagram, bottom page 57).

Hold the upper part of the shaker by its tenon in compression mode and face off. Drill a 1 in. (25 mm) hole to a depth of ⅜ in. (10 mm). Referring to the main diagram opposite, use the recess tool to turn a rebate at the base of the hole to act as the run-off for the female thread chaser. Dome the bottom of the drilled hole as before. Chase the female thread.

Now is a good time to start the partial bead on the outside of this part of the shaker. It will be more difficult to sweep round to the thread when the two halves are screwed together. After removing the top half from the lathe, drill the ¹⁄₁₆ in. (1.5 mm) exit holes through the tenon as before.

Remount the bottom half of the shaker and reduce the top tenon diameter to 1¹⁄₁₆ in. (27 mm). Form a small chamfer on the top

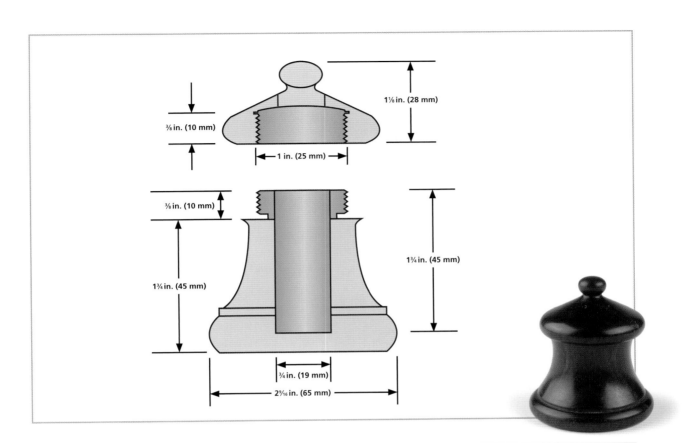

of the tenon. Use a small parting tool to form a recess at the bottom of the tenon, which will act as the run-off point for the thread chaser. Now start to chase the male thread. Continue chasing the thread until you have a smooth action between the male and female threads.

Drill the reservoir ¾ in. (19 mm) in diameter by 1¾ in. (45 mm) deep.

Screw the two halves together and shape the outside of the Bell. Keep the tailstock in place until the top of the Bell is about to be turned. As before, a small round-ended scraper is useful to turn the curve on the underside of the knob.

Remount the base on a ¾ in. (19 mm) jam chuck. Ensure that it is running true. Remove the tenon and clean up the base, leaving it slightly concave. Sand and finish the whole Bell. I recommend an oil-based finish for this wood.

> ▶ **HINT:**
> If the first pass at chasing the male thread fails, part off the thread tenon. Drill a 1⅛ in. (28 mm) hole to a depth of ¾ in. (19 mm). Turn up a new tenon from the same wood, glue this in, and try again.

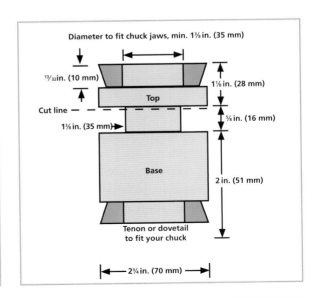

Diameter to fit chuck jaws, min. 1⅜ in. (35 mm)

¹³⁄₃₂ in. (10 mm)

Cut line —

Top

1⅛ in. (28 mm)

⅝ in. (16 mm)

1⅜ in. (35 mm)

Base

2 in. (51 mm)

Tenon or dovetail to fit your chuck

2¾ in. (70 mm)

7 SEMICIRCULAR

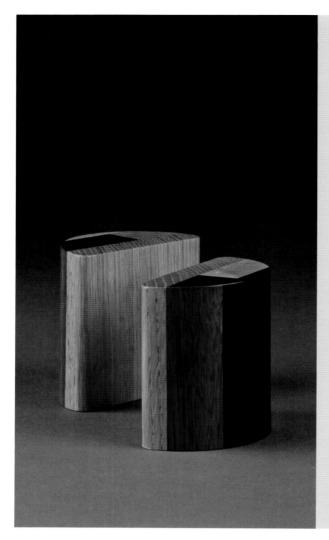

■ Level of difficulty: **Experienced**

TOOLS
¾ in. (19 mm) spindle roughing gouge
⅜ in. (10 mm) spindle gouge
⅛ in. (3 mm) parting tool

Accessories required: Bung

WOOD
Oak, box, ebony, bloodwood, pau amarello

Height: 3⅜ in. (85 mm)
Diameter: 3⅛ in. (80 mm)
Blank dimensions: See diagram for widths and thicknesses. Length for a pair of shakers is 4⅛ in. (105 mm). This allows for facing off and for a holding tenon.

This project attempts to create appealing patterns by laminating a number of different woods. You might turn a prototype from a single piece of scrap hardwood to ascertain the height and diameter you prefer. You could consider using longer lengths of wood to make several pairs of shakers.

All of the blank pieces must be accurately planed and thicknessed before gluing. The woods are initially glued and clamped as two individual blanks for the salt and pepper shakers. When dry, the two back faces are planed and the two halves glued together with brown paper between them, using white PVA glue.

The square blank is then turned to a cylinder and sanded. The pairs of shakers are parted to the chosen length using the ⅛ in. (3 mm) parting tool or a bandsaw. The two shakers are then carefully split in two using a wide woodworker's chisel driven in at the end where a tenon or dovetail will be turned.

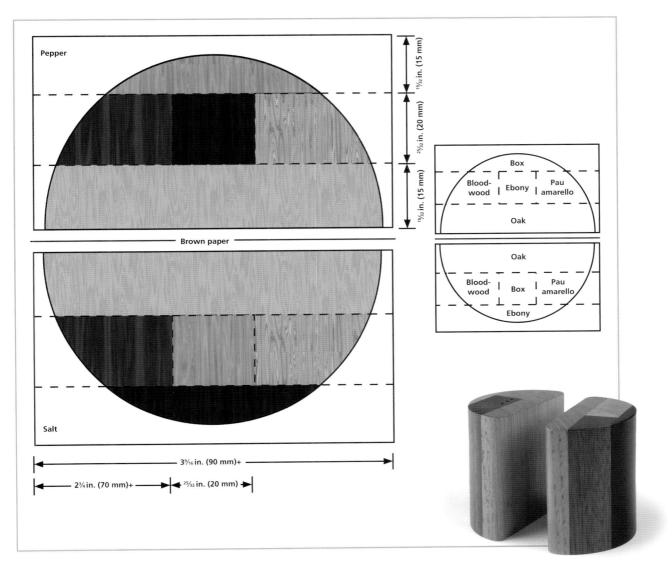

The center point of the semicircular shaker must now be marked at each end. To do this, measure halfway across the flat side and draw a line at 90° to the flat side, then find the midpoint of this line. Note that this is not in the center of the box and ebony square pieces; centering the holes on these would leave the outer bung hole very near the edge of the shaker. The shaker is now mounted between centers and a tenon or dovetail is turned to fit your lathe jaws.

Mount the tenon in compression mode and, when running true, drill the bung hole. A ¾ in. (19 mm) bung fits these shakers admirably. Measure the length required for the reservoir, and mark this on the drill bit's shaft before drilling; if you are making your shakers 3⅜ in. (85 mm) high, drill the reservoir hole 3³⁄₁₆ in. (81 mm) deep. An ¹¹⁄₁₆ in. (17.5 mm) hole can be drilled to accommodate both the bung and the reservoir. Remove from the lathe and cut off the tenon using a bandsaw. A belt sander is best suited for sanding the shakers to remove traces of the brown paper.

After a final sanding by hand, seal and spray the shakers with an acrylic gloss lacquer, before final buffing using a micro-abrasive polishing compound and, finally, carnauba wax. The exit holes for the salt and pepper are marked and drilled using a ¹⁄₁₆ in. (1.5 mm) twist drill.

8 HAT

■ Level of difficulty: **Intermediate**

TOOLS
¾ in. (19 mm) spindle roughing gouge
½ in. (13 mm) spindle gouge
½ in. (13 mm) beading and parting tool
½ in. (13 mm) skew chisel
½ in. (13 mm) round-nosed scraper
⅛ in. (3 mm) parting tool

Accessories required: Bung

WOOD
Pink ivory; rosewood insert

Height: 3⅜ in. (86 mm)
Diameter: 2¹/₁₆ in. (52 mm)
Blank dimensions:
Combined body and top: 2³/₁₆ x 2³/₁₆ x 3⅞ in.
(56 x 56 x 98 mm)
Insert: 1 x 1 x 1¼ in. (25 x 25 x 32 mm)
These dimensions allow for facing off
and for tenons or dovetails, which will
be mostly incorporated into the shaker
as the project proceeds.

These shakers are turned from pink ivory, which can be very expensive, even for just an offcut! With this in mind, I had to use the minimum amount for the blank, so I incorporated the tenon or dovetail into the shaker as much as possible.

The diagram opposite gives the dimensions for the shaker and the blank, which I managed to fit into a piece of pink ivory I had. The pepper shaker has a rosewood insert.

Rough-turn to a cylinder. Mark out the two sections, turn the dovetail and spigot, and part using a bandsaw.

BODY
Mount the body by its tenon in compression jaws and face off the base. Drill the two holes for the bung. The ²³/₃₂ in. (18 mm) hole should only be drilled to a depth of 2³/₁₆ in. (56 mm).

If necessary, open the larger hole at the bottom to allow easy access to the bung.

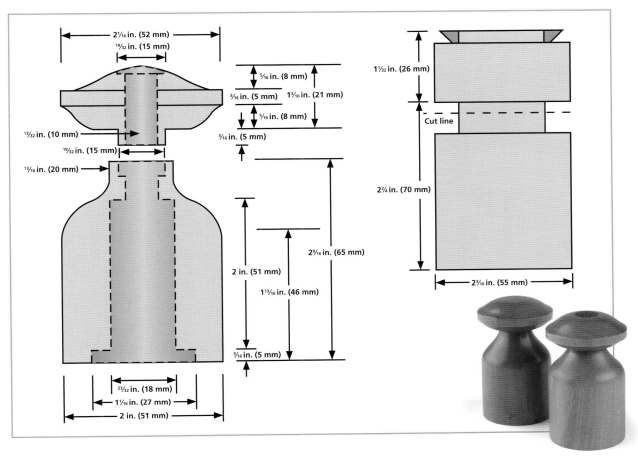

Reverse, holding the base in expansion jaws. Part off to a length of 2⁹⁄₁₆ in. (65 mm). Drill a ¹³⁄₃₂ in. (10 mm) hole to meet the reservoir hole drilled previously. Using a ½ in. (13 mm) skew, open the ¹³⁄₃₂ in. (10 mm) hole to ¹⁹⁄₃₂ in. (15 mm), ³⁄₁₆ in. (5 mm) deep. Remove from the lathe and support the body between a cone-shaped jam chuck and a cone center in the tailstock to shape the outside. Sand down to 400 grit and seal.

TOP

Mount the top by its dovetail in compression jaws, ensuring it runs true. Face off and drill a ¹³⁄₃₂ in. (10 mm) hole all the way through for the pepper and ³⁄₁₆ in. (5 mm) short of the top for the salt shaker. Turn the spigot to be a good fit into the base.

Mark out the three key distances along the length of the top. Turn the lower curve as shown, sand and seal. Reverse, holding the spigot in compression jaws.

For the salt shaker, shape the top curve and use a ¹⁄₁₆ in. (1.5 mm) twist drill held in a Jacobs chuck to drill the exit hole for the salt. For the pepper shaker, open the ¹³⁄₃₂ in. (10 mm) hole to a width of ¹⁹⁄₃₂ in. (15 mm) for a depth of ⁵⁄₃₂ in. (4 mm). Turn the top curve as shown, sand, and seal. Remove the top from the lathe.

INSERT (PEPPER SHAKER ONLY)

Turn a ¹⁹⁄₃₂ in. (15 mm) insert, ¼ in. (6 mm) long, to be a tight fit in the top. Mark and drill the three exit holes before gluing it into the top and completing the final shaping.

ASSEMBLY AND FINISHING

The top is now glued into the base. Try to line up the grain between the two halves.

I chose to spray the shakers using acrylic lacquer, but they could have had an oil finish. They were de-nibbed between coats and buffed to give a beautiful sheen.

9 MUFFINEER

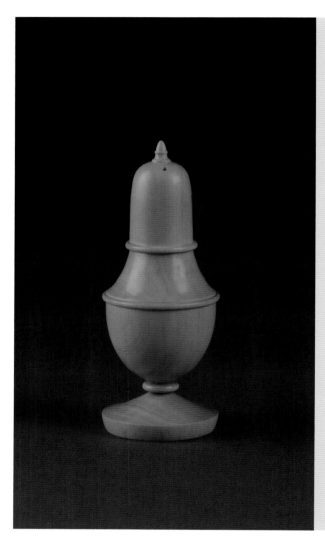

TOOLS
¾ in. (19 mm) spindle roughing gouge
⅛ in. (3 mm) miniature spindle gouge
¼ in. (6 mm) miniature spindle gouge
⅜ in. (10 mm) spindle gouge
⅜ in. (10 mm) miniature flat skew chisel
½ in. (13 mm) skew chisel
½ in. (13 mm) beading and parting tool
1/16 in. (1.5 mm) parting tool
⅛ in. (3 mm) parting tool
Recess tool
19 tpi thread chasers

Accessories required: None

WOOD
Box

Height: 5⁵/16 in. (135 mm)
Diameter: 2⅛ in. (54 mm)
Blank dimensions: *Body and lid for each shaker:*
2½ x 2½ x 6½ in. (60 x 64 x 165 mm)
For both threaded inserts: a single piece
1³/16 x 1³/16 x 2 in. (30 x 30 x 51 mm)

This shaker is of the traditional "muffineer" type, described on page 28. It is in two parts; unscrewing the top gives access to the salt reservoir. The male and female screw threads are formed as two separate inserts, to simplify the thread-chasing procedure.

BASE
After rough-turning between centers, cut the blank into two and hold the base of the shaker by its tenon or dovetail in your chuck jaws, initially with the tailstock in place to ensure that it is running true. Face off the base to the correct length, ensuring that the end face is square. Hollow the inside as shown in the diagram. This is a good time to turn the top 1¼ in. (32 mm) bead on the base.

Either make up a jam chuck to fit inside the reservoir, or hold the reservoir opening in expansion jaws with the tailstock in place. Ensure that it is running true. Remove the tenon at the base and finish the bottom of the shaker.

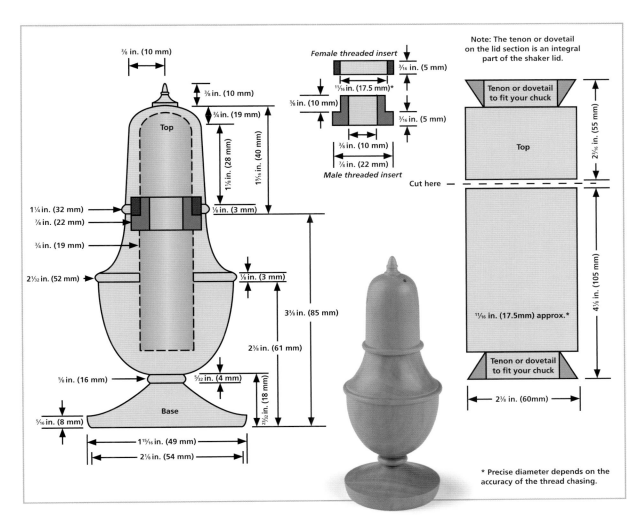

TOP

Mount the blank for the top in your chuck by means of its tenon or dovetail, and drill and shape the inside as shown in the diagram. The outside is also turned in this position, except for the very top of the shaker. Remove from the lathe, reverse, and, using expansion jaws to hold the top section by its base, finish turning the top of the shaker. Don't forget that the material used for the tenon or dovetail becomes part of the finished top.

FEMALE THREAD INSERT

The blank dimensions given allow sufficient wood for both the male and female inserts and a holding tenon. Drill a ¹⁹⁄₃₂ in. (15 mm) hole into the blank to a depth of about ¾ in. (19 mm) before reducing its outside diameter—that is, while the diameter is still 1³⁄₁₆ in. (30 mm). This

will allow room for error in order to finish with a female thread approximately ¹¹⁄₁₆ in. (17.5 mm) in diameter. Hand-chase the female thread and reduce the outside to ⅞ in. (22 mm) diameter, ensuring that it is a good fit in the shaker top. Part off the insert to ³⁄₁₆ in. (5 mm) long.

MALE THREAD INSERT

Reduce the diameter for the threaded section to ¾ in. (19 mm) and chase the male thread before drilling the just over ⁹⁄₁₆ in. (15 mm) hole through. Finally, reduce the outside to a diameter of ⅞ in. (22 mm) and remove the tenon, leaving an overall length of ⅜ in. (10 mm).

When the two inserts are screwed together, they should be a close fit. If all looks good, the two inserts can be glued into the shaker base and top respectively. Finish as desired.

10 UPSIDE-DOWN

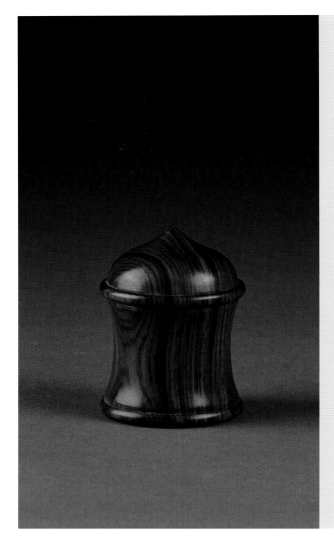

TOOLS

¾ in. (19 mm) spindle roughing gouge
⅜ in. (10 mm) spindle gouge
½ in. (13 mm) round-nosed scraper
½ in. (13 mm) beading and parting tool
⅛ in. (3 mm) parting tool
³⁄₁₆ in. (5 mm) fluted parting tool

Accessories required: None

WOOD

Cocobolo

Height: 3¼ in. (83 mm)
Diameter: 2¼ in. (57 mm)
Blank dimensions: 2½ x 2½ x 6½ in.
(64 x 64 x 165 mm)
These dimensions include sufficient wood
for both parts of the shaker and a holding
tenon or dovetail.

The principle of this shaker is that when you shake it, salt falls out through the bottom, but on returning it to the upright—nothing!

When the shaker is shaken, the salt that was lying in the bottom of the chamber bounces off the dome at the top of the chamber and some will fall through the central tube. The only critical dimension is the distance between the tube and the dome: it must be ½ in. (13 mm).

BODY

Mount the blank between centers and rough-turn to a cylinder, turning a tenon or dovetail at one end. Face off the base and, using a 1½ in. (38 mm) Forstner bit, drill in approximately 1⅝ in. (41 mm) —this is not a critical measurement. Using a ½ in. (13 mm) round-nosed scraper, turn a dome in the top. Using a beading and parting tool, turn a ⅛ in. (3 mm) wide step, ⅛ in. (3 mm) deep in the base. Mark out the dimensions for the body. Turn the bottom bead at this time. Part the shaker off.

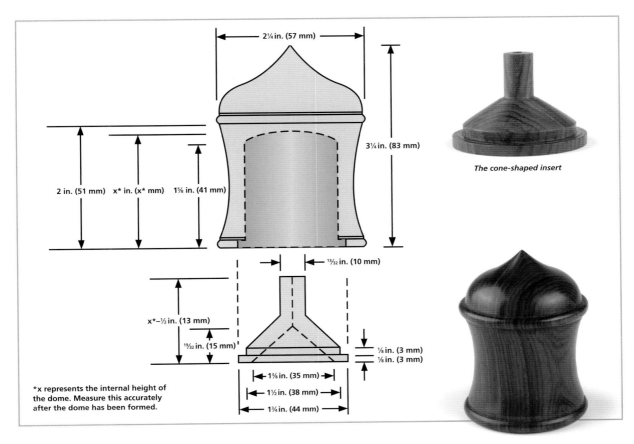

2¼ in. (57 mm)

3¼ in. (83 mm)

2 in. (51 mm)   x* in. (x* mm)   1⅝ in. (41 mm)

¹³⁄₃₂ in. (10 mm)

x*−½ in. (13 mm)

¹⁹⁄₃₂ in. (15 mm)

⅛ in. (3 mm)
⅛ in. (3 mm)

1⅜ in. (35 mm)

1½ in. (38 mm)

1¾ in. (44 mm)

*x represents the internal height of
the dome. Measure this accurately
after the dome has been formed.

The cone-shaped insert

INSERT

Face off the remaining part of the blank,
and form an internal funnel 1⅜ in. (35 mm)
diameter and ¹⁹⁄₃₂ in. (15 mm) deep into the
end. Using a Jacobs drill chuck in the tailstock,
drill a hole 1⅛ in. (28 mm) deep; the drill size
should be ⁵⁄₆₄ in. (2 mm) for fine table salt; for
fine sea salt, it should be up to ⅛ in. (3 mm).

Turn the outside diameter of 1¾ in. (44 mm) to
fit the shaker's base. Keep checking and offering
up the shaker to ensure that a good fit is
obtained. Next, turn the step, which will be ⅛ in.
(3 mm) wide and should equal the diameter of
the inside of the shaker—1½ in. (38 mm). The
remaining wood is now turned to this diameter.
With a cone center in the tailstock, taper the
outside of the funnel to a shaft ¹³⁄₃₂ in. (10 mm)
in diameter.

Use a depth gauge to accurately measure the
depth of the hole in the main body of the
shaker to the center of the dome. Subtract ½ in.

(13 mm) from this and mark out the length on
the insert as shown. Withdraw the tailstock and
part off to this length as squarely as possible.

Sand the stem and the outside of the funnel. Do
not apply any finish where it may touch the salt.

FINAL STAGES

The insert should fit snugly into the base. Before
gluing together, pour a little salt in through the
base and, holding the insert in place, shake the
shaker to confirm that the correct amount of salt
emerges. Re-drill the hole if necessary.

Mount the shaker either on a jam chuck or in
expansion jaws. Bring the tailstock up to give
support and proceed to turn the body to its
final shape. If you are using expansion jaws,
you will now see why the bottom bead was
turned earlier. After shaping and sanding,
finish as required. Glue the insert in place with
cyanoacrylate (Super Glue) and buff using White
Diamond and a coat of Renaissance wax.

MILLS

DESIGNING MILLS

Before considering how to design a mill, it is important to clarify the terminology that we will be using in the sections that follow. To help with this, the illustration below highlights the key descriptive words for the mill itself.

The *top* and *main body* are self-explanatory. Physically there is no difference between a *spigot* and a *tenon*, but I use "spigot" to refer to an integral part of the mill, and "tenon" to describe a piece that is there only for you to hold the wood during turning, and which will be removed before the mill is complete. The top tenon can be replaced by a dovetail, depending on the chuck jaws available to you.

You may already have an idea of the shape and height you want for your mill, and even the wood you would like to use. If the mill is intended for someone else, they may have stated their requirements, in which case there is little flexibility. For this exercise, let's assume that you're making the mill for yourself. The world is your oyster!

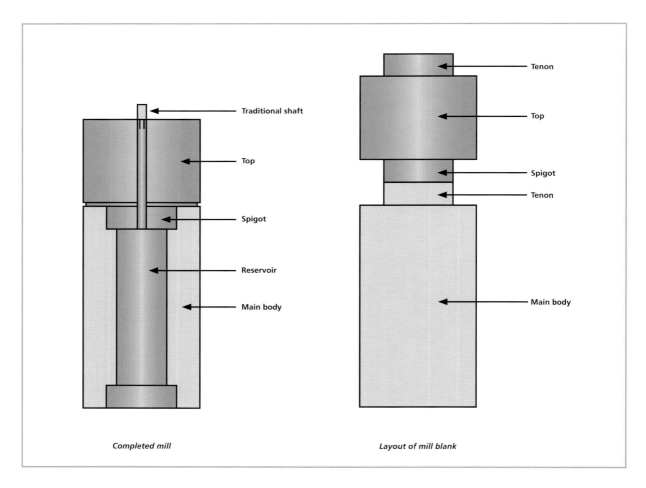

Completed mill   *Layout of mill blank*

There are two types of mechanisms used in mills:

The traditional mechanism

The CrushGrind® mechanism

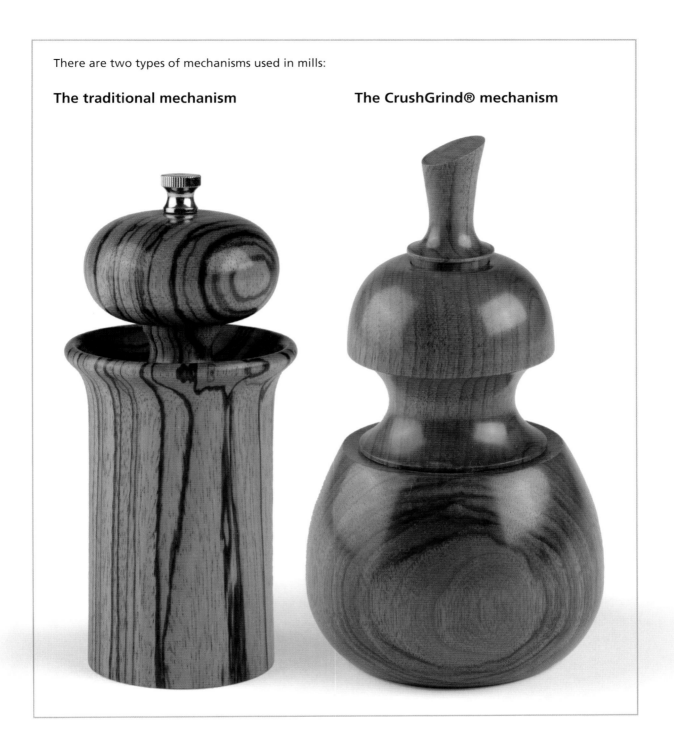

The traditional mill uses a finial nut or knurled knob to attach the top to the main body and for grinding adjustment. While the CrushGrind® does not need a finial nut, a knurled nut at the base of the mill controls the grinding action.

As part of the design process, it is important to consider the minimum allowable diameters of the mill, given the mechanisms available. The diagrams on page 71–73 give an indication of the minimum sizes at various points on the mill, which will assist in choosing the correct mechanism for your design.

It is now time to examine the mechanisms that are available.

CHOOSING A MILL MECHANISM

There are a number of quality salt and pepper mechanisms being manufactured around the world. However, only a few are available for purchase by individual woodturners. Those mentioned here can be bought as mechanisms alone, but others may be available in your area. Details of suppliers are to be found on pages 168–169.

There are two basic types of traditional salt and pepper mechanisms, examples of which are shown below and opposite. The traditional mechanism relies on a finial nut or knurled knob at the top of the mill, while the CrushGrind® has an adjustment nut at the base of the mill.

At present, the longest mill shaft readily available to the woodturner is 20 in. (510 mm).

TRADITIONAL MECHANISMS

Throughout this book I will be referring to traditional mechanisms as either Type 1 or Type 2 mechanisms. Type 1 refers to a particular type of mechanism, which is sourced in the UK, while Type 2 is commonly available in North America. The photographs below and opposite show the components of these mechanisms, while the line diagrams show the minimum diameters needed

for a mill to accommodate these mechanisms. Consult the stockists listed on pages 168–9 for the suppliers of traditional Type 1 and Type 2 mechanisms.

Both Type 1 and 2 pepper-grinding mechanisms are made from hardened stainless steel, while the salt mechanisms are molded from hardened plastic. It is important to ensure that stainless-steel screws are used to secure the salt mechanisms. They can also be used for the pepper mechanisms, but you will often find that zinc-plated steel screws are supplied with the pepper mechanism.

Some manufacturers produce mechanisms made from ceramic material that can be used for both salt and pepper.

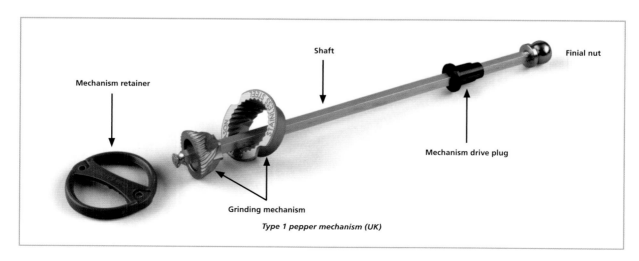

Mechanism retainer

Shaft

Finial nut

Mechanism drive plug

Grinding mechanism

Type 1 pepper mechanism (UK)

Differences between Type 1 and Type 2 mechanisms

Type 1 mechanisms are supplied with two self-adhesive circular labels marked **S** and **P**, which are pressed onto the supplied finial nuts.

Some **Type 2** mechanisms have an **S** or **P** already engraved on the top of the final nut. Make sure the appropriately engraved finial nut is screwed to each mill!

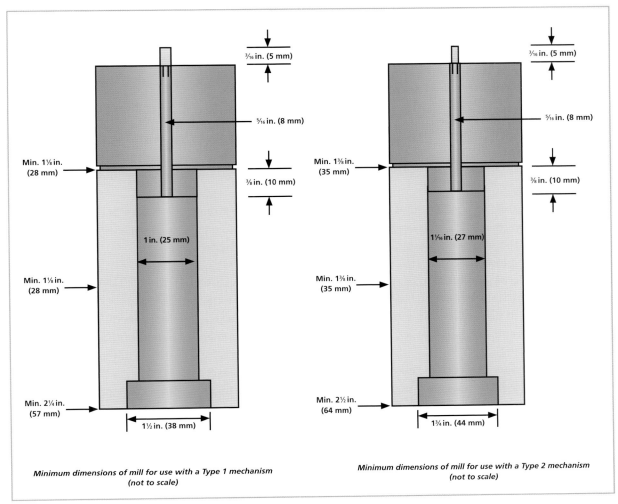

Minimum dimensions of mill for use with a Type 1 mechanism (not to scale)

Minimum dimensions of mill for use with a Type 2 mechanism (not to scale)

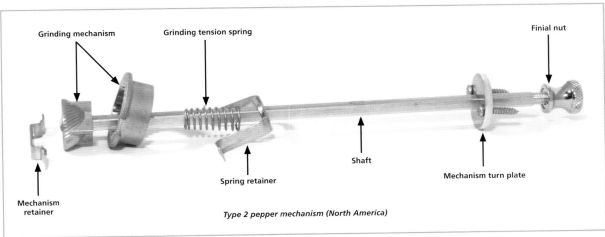

Type 2 pepper mechanism (North America)

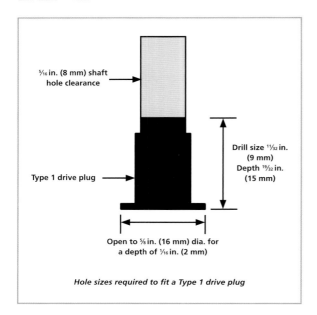

5⁄16 in. (8 mm) shaft
hole clearance

Drill size ¹¹⁄₃₂ in.
(9 mm)
Depth ¹⁹⁄₃₂ in.
(15 mm)

Type 1 drive plug

Open to ⅝ in. (16 mm) dia. for
a depth of ¹⁄₁₆ in. (2 mm)

Hole sizes required to fit a Type 1 drive plug

This leads me to stress how important it is to identify clearly which mill is for the salt and which for the pepper. Other ways of achieving this are: dark or light wood inserts incorporated into the top of the mill; the use of laser burning or engraving to inscribe the words "Salt" or "Pepper" onto the mill; your own design of finial nuts using contrasting woods and insert nuts (see pages 74–77).

Recently the manager of an ocean beach restaurant asked me why his pepper-mill mechanisms were going rusty. It turned out that the restaurant staff had been putting salt in the mill intended for pepper, which had a hardened steel mechanism, not one made from stainless steel. They were also putting pepper into the mill with a hardened plastic grinding mechanism and wondering why the grinding mechanisms were not lasting long. The staff compounded the problem by screwing the finial nuts onto the wrong mill. As you can imagine, both the customers and the staff of the restaurant were getting very confused.

MECHANISM DRIVE PLUG AND PLATE

Type 1 mechanisms use a plastic drive plug made with a square hole through it; the plug has "wings" on the side that compress when driven into the ¹¹⁄₃₂ in. (9 mm) hole in the base of the spigot.

Type 2 mechanisms have a ¹⁵⁄₁₆ in. (24 mm) circular turn plate with a ³⁄₁₆ in. (5 mm) square hole punched through the aluminum. This is fixed with two screws into the base of the spigot.

GRIND ADJUSTMENT

The **Type 1** grinding mechanism relies on finial-nut tension to adjust the grind.

Type 2 has a spring above the grinding mechanism that creates tension on the mechanism when the finial nut is tightened.

SHAFT SIZE AND THREAD

The **Type 1** shaft is made from 5 mm square aluminum and has a metric M5 thread at the top.

Many **Type 2** shafts are made from ³⁄₁₆ in. square aluminum and have an Imperial UNC ⁷⁄₃₂ in., 12 x 24 thread at the top.

CRUSHGRIND® SHAFT MECHANISMS

In 1992, the Danish company IDEAS®, along with a Japanese inventor called Kamioka, began the development of a multipurpose ceramic grinder for all spices. This resulted in the very successful mechanism known as the CrushGrind®, which can be used for grinding both sea salt and peppercorns. There are two varieties: shaft mechanisms and wood mechanisms.

▶ **WEAR AND TEAR**

If you look closely at the actual grinding parts of any of the mechanisms mentioned above, you will see that the mill top should be turned in a clockwise direction to grind the salt or pepper.

Many TV chefs can be seen twisting the top backwards and forwards—this isn't the correct way! It looks good, but the grinding mechanism will wear out sooner. But of course celebrity chefs can afford to replace them at their whim.

CrushGrind® shaft mechanisms

The top portion of the CrushGrind® can be moved along the aluminum shaft as required, and the shaft can be shortened as necessary using a hacksaw and cleaned up with a file. Adjustment to the grind is facilitated by the knurled knob at the base of the mechanism. The diagram below shows the minimum diameters a mill requires for this mechanism. See page 132 for details of the diameter and depth of holes to be drilled.

CrushGrind® wood mechanisms

It is not easy to see in a photograph, but the top half with the spring clips revolves when the bottom half is fixed in the base of the mill. The grinding adjustment is the same as for the CrushGrind® shaft mechanism. The diagram below shows the minimum diameters a mill requires for this mechanism. See page 132 for details of the diameter and depth of holes to be drilled.

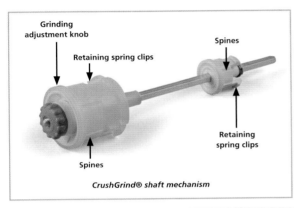

CrushGrind® shaft mechanism

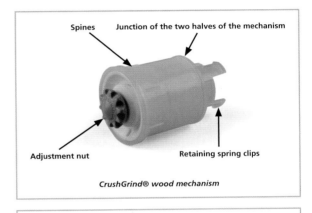

CrushGrind® wood mechanism

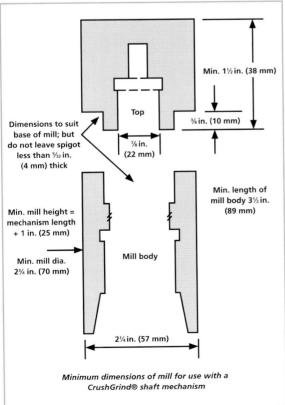

Minimum dimensions of mill for use with a CrushGrind® shaft mechanism

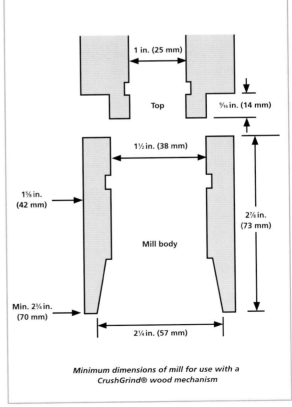

Minimum dimensions of mill for use with a CrushGrind® wood mechanism

MILL FINIAL NUTS

Although the finial nuts supplied with the grinder mechanism are perfectly adequate, you may find it more satisfying to design and turn your own finial nuts. This section will give you the necessary information to achieve this.

Type 1 finial nuts with self-adhesive labels applied

Just to recap: glue-backed circular labels with an **S** and a **P** are supplied with Type 1 mechanisms. The user is responsible for sticking the labels onto the finial nuts. This finial nut has an M5 thread.

With the Type 2 mechanism, the letters **S** and **P** are often engraved on the top of the finial nut. This finial nut has a $^7/_{32}$ in., 12 x 24 UNC thread.

In both types, the purpose of the finial nut is to allow some degree of adjustment as to the fineness of the salt and pepper. With the Type 2 mechanism this objective is enhanced by the use of a spring to regulate the tension placed on the grinding mechanism.

SLOTTED-SCREW FINIAL NUTS

Proprietary finial nuts are great for traditional-shaped mills, but other types of finial can extend your design capabilities. For example, my Chianti bottle (Project 16, pages 106–107) uses a recessed finial nut that does not spoil the outline of the design. A slot for a screwdriver or teaspoon in the top of the nut allows for adjustment.

If you have access to an engineering lathe, you can make this item yourself from aluminum, to the dimensions given below. Alternatively, small quantities for Type 1 and Type 2 are available from the author; see page 169 for contact details.

An engraved finial nut from a Type 2 mechanism

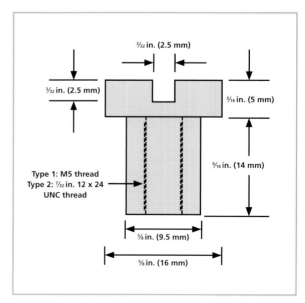

Type 1: M5 thread
Type 2: $^7/_{32}$ in. 12 x 24 UNC thread

$^3/_{32}$ in. (2.5 mm)
$^3/_{32}$ in. (2.5 mm)
$^3/_{16}$ in. (5 mm)
$^9/_{16}$ in. (14 mm)
$^3/_8$ in. (9.5 mm)
$^5/_8$ in. (16 mm)

Dimensions of the slotted-screw finial nut

A slotted-screw finial nut

This slightly smaller, chrome-plated version is available in M5 only; see pages 168–169 for supplier details

THREADED INSERT (DOGTOOTH) NUTS
TYPE 1

The Type 1 mechanism has an M5 thread on its shaft. A zinc-plated insert nut with the same thread can be used as part of a turned wooden finial nut made to your own design, as in Project 21 (pages 120–122). Insert nuts are available from many suppliers of screws, nuts and fixing hardware. If you cannot find a local supplier, check online retailers.

The spigot of the wooden finial nut needs to be drilled to a size that is large enough to eliminate the chance of the wood cracking when the insert nut is pressed in, but small enough to ensure that the teeth of the nut still bind onto the wood. Experiment on scrap wood until you are happy with the chosen drill size; I find a 5⁄16 in. (8 mm) drill suits the nuts I use. The insert nut can be gently knocked into the spigot. I apply two-part epoxy glue to the teeth prior to tapping them in; this ensures that the insert nut cannot turn within the wood. To be absolutely honest I am not sure whether the epoxy is essential, but I have always used it and found that it works well.

Threaded insert (dogtooth) nut for Type 1 mechanism

Chianti bottle mill, using a recessed slot-headed finial nut

A turned finial nut with an insert nut embedded in it to form the female thread

TYPE 2

The thread on the Type 2 shaft is $^7/_{32}$ in., 12 x 24 UNC. Nuts of this type can be supplied by the author in small quantities. An alternative is to drill out and retap an M5 insert nut to fit the thread on the shaft of your grinding mechanism.

If you are making a pair of mills, it is strongly advised that you use contrasting woods for the salt and pepper, because you won't be able to tell which is which from the finial nuts.

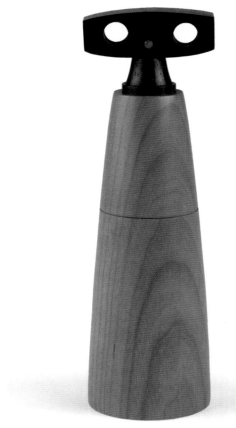

Threaded insert (dogtooth) nut for Type 2 mechanism

The Alien invader mill (see pages 120–2)

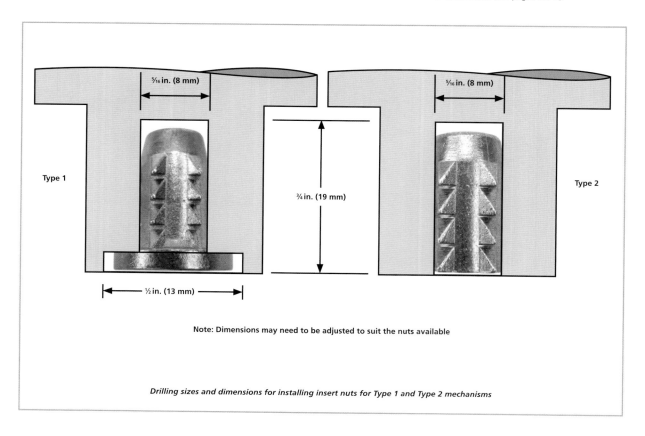

Type 1

Type 2

$^5/_{16}$ in. (8 mm)

$^5/_{16}$ in. (8 mm)

$^3/_4$ in. (19 mm)

$^1/_2$ in. (13 mm)

Note: Dimensions may need to be adjusted to suit the nuts available

Drilling sizes and dimensions for installing insert nuts for Type 1 and Type 2 mechanisms

DESIGN OPTIONS

Project 21 on pages 120–122 shows two approaches to utilizing insert nuts.

Until now, I have been talking about the insert nut as an integral part of a wooden finial nut. However, other materials can be used:

Polyester resin: comes in many colors and patterns. It can be tapped, but I have concerns about the durability of the tapped thread. Alternatively, an insert nut can be glued in.

Metal: brass, bronze, and stainless steel are just three of the metals that can be used to make finial nuts. You may need the help of a friend with mechanical engineering machinery if you don't have the skills and equipment yourself. There is an example of a brass finial nut in the Gallery (page 166).

If you consider the finial nut to be an integral part of your final design, you can allow your imagination to run wild!

FINALIZING A MILL DESIGN

Let's assume that your mill will use a traditional mechanism but that no final decision has yet been made with regard to the finial nut. The process of drawing up the mill design is similar to that for the shaker, only more detail is needed.

COMMON DESIGN CONSIDERATIONS

Start your design on a piece of squared paper. As you can see from the first sketch below, I only wanted to get some idea of the balance between the height and the width.

Once the height of the mill has been decided, based on the shaft lengths of the available mechanisms, draw to scale on squared paper the holes to be drilled for your chosen mechanism.

If your design cannot be adjusted to fit an available shaft length, then the shaft can be shortened quite easily (see pages 88–9).

Will the supplied finial nut look right with your design, or should you turn your own, using an insert nut? The Alien invader design shown opposite would be pointless without using a custom-made nut. But for the time being let's assume that you have decided to use the supplied finial nut.

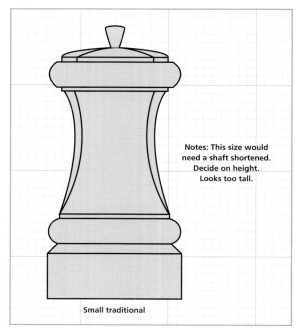

Notes: This size would need a shaft shortened. Decide on height. Looks too tall.

Small traditional

A first rough sketch to assess the proportions

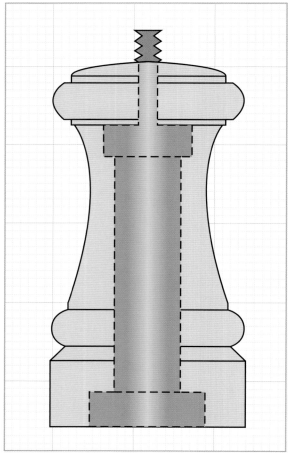

The second sketch incorporates the holes needed to fit the mechanism

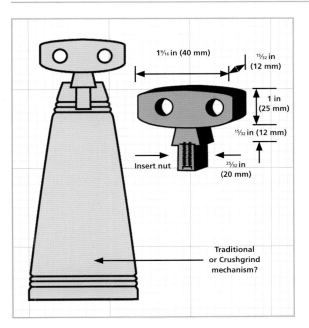

The Alien Invader mill design cries out for a purpose-made nut

1⁹⁄₁₆ in (40 mm)

¹⁵⁄₃₂ in (12 mm)

1 in (25 mm)

¹⁵⁄₃₂ in (12 mm)

²⁵⁄₃₂ in (20 mm)

Insert nut

Traditional or Crushgrind mechanism?

THE PROTOTYPE

The initial shape is turned between centers from softwood or an unwanted piece of hardwood. No holes are drilled other than a ¼ in. (6 mm) hole in the top, into which will go a finial nut attached to a 1 in. (25 mm) length of M5 or ³⁄₁₆ in. studding.

The photographs below offer an example of the kind of correction you might make at this stage: the second version has been made a little wider at the base to give a better balance.

Don't be afraid to seek a second opinion. Make adjustments to your prototype, or, if necessary, add it to the firewood pile and start again. When you are happy with the look of the mill, update your diagram accordingly and add the dimensions. Also make a diagram of the blank, allowing for the additional wood required for parting off, and mounting tenons and a locating spigot.

The prototype sprayed matte black

The first prototype looks top-heavy

A slightly broader base makes the second version look more stable

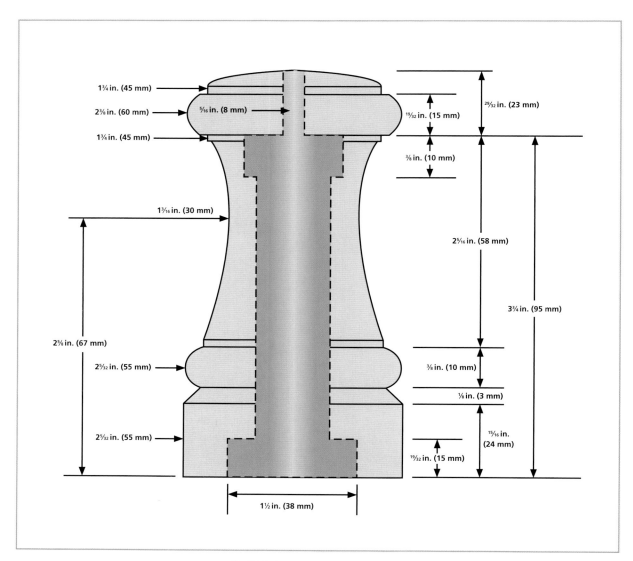

1¾ in. (45 mm)

2⅜ in. (60 mm) ⁵⁄₁₆ in. (8 mm)

1¾ in. (45 mm)

1³⁄₁₆ in. (30 mm)

2⅝ in. (67 mm)

2⁵⁄₃₂ in. (55 mm)

2⁵⁄₃₂ in. (55 mm)

1½ in. (38 mm)

²⁹⁄₃₂ in. (23 mm)

¹⁹⁄₃₂ in. (15 mm)

⅜ in. (10 mm)

2⁵⁄₁₆ in. (58 mm)

3¾ in. (95 mm)

⅜ in. (10 mm)

⅛ in. (3 mm)

¹⁵⁄₁₆ in. (24 mm)

¹⁹⁄₃₂ in. (15 mm)

The finished diagram with dimensions added

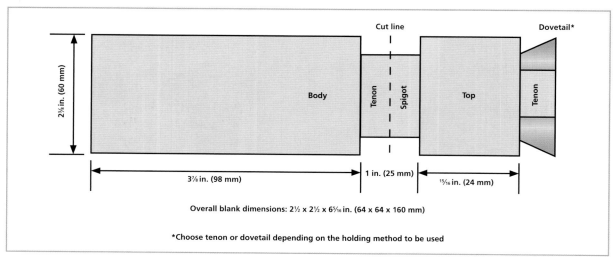

Cut line

Dovetail*

2⅜ in. (60 mm)

Body

Tenon

Spigot

Top

Tenon

3⅞ in. (98 mm)

1 in. (25 mm)

¹⁵⁄₁₆ in. (24 mm)

Overall blank dimensions: 2½ x 2½ x 6⁵⁄₁₆ in. (64 x 64 x 160 mm)

*Choose tenon or dovetail depending on the holding method to be used

Sketch showing blank dimensions

LOCATING SPIGOTS

The spigot is the locator between the top and the body (see page 68). There are two options:

Option 1: The spigot sits in a recess which is wider than the reservoir. An advantage of this method is the salt or pepper is easier to pour into the mill.

Option 2: The spigot is the same size as the reservoir. The length of the spigot should be no more than approximately ⅜ in. (10 mm) long so that only a small amount of grain is lost on the outside. This ensures a more seamless flow between the body and top of the mill. This option also reduces the amount of drilling you will need to do. Professional turners usually use Option 2 in order to reduce the time taken to turn the mill.

CHOICE OF WOOD

If the client has asked for a particular type of wood, you may well have taken that into account when you designed the mill.

If the client has no idea—which is quite understandable—you may need to ask some further questions, such as:

Do you prefer the wood to be dark or light?

Are the mills intended to enhance the dining-table layout on special occasions?

If they are for daily use in the kitchen, are there any height restrictions?

Does the client want them to blend with existing furniture?

Are the mills a gift?

You can then recommend a wood that you know is available and that you think may meet the client's criteria.

If the choice of wood is yours, it is worth looking carefully at the design to see whether it lends itself to the grain pattern of a particular wood. For ideas on woods, see pages 18–21.

If a particularly attractively grained wood has been identified, you may want the grain in the mill's body and top to flow seamlessly into each other. To achieve this you can make a separate spigot in the same wood and fit this into a pre-drilled hole in the mill top. This way, the discontinuity in the grain will be no greater than the thickness of your parting tool. Don't forget to include this in the diagram of the blank, to remind you that the spigot can also be taken from another part of the plank.

RESIZING A MILL

Let's say you have made a 6 in. (152 mm) mill, and a customer would like one to the same design but 8 in. (203 mm) high. You might think of simply scaling up your whole design by 33%, but this will rarely work: the diameters will usually look too big. You need to redraw the mill to scale until, to your eye, all the dimensions are in proportion. I recommend that you make a new prototype before beginning to turn the client's mill.

TURNING A TRADITIONAL MILL

This section takes you through the process of turning a mill. It covers holding and drilling methods, how to fit a mechanism, and how to shorten a mechanism. I will assume that you have made a prototype and detailed dimensional diagrams as described in the previous section, and that you have a suitable mechanism.

CHOICE OF WOOD

Help with your choice of wood type was given on pages 18–21. Beware of knots in the blank unless you are confident at dealing with knots and want to make them a feature. It is imperative that the wood you are going to use for your mill is dry; otherwise, movement after turning will lead to a spigot going oval, causing difficulty in twisting the top.

HOLDING THE TURNED BLANKS

The blank can be held in a number of different ways. Which method you use may well depend on the jaws you have available. The options are:

JUMBO COMPRESSION JAWS

These jaws, provided they have enough capacity, can be used to hold the outside diameter of the blank. A big advantage is that jumbo jaws are strong enough to hold a longer blank that is possibly going to be drilled from both ends. Never extend the jaws to the maximum, to avoid the risk of one or more of the individual jaws flying out when the lathe is turned on.

SMALLER COMPRESSION JAWS

These can be used to hold a tenon formed on the workpiece, or a custom-made jam chuck. A tenon with a diameter of approximately 1⅝ in. (40 mm) and ⅝ in. (15 mm) long will hold a blank more than 6 in. (152 mm) long so that it can be comfortably drilled. But the warning about never extending your chuck jaws to the maximum still applies.

Four-jaw scroll chucks fitted with O'Donnell jaws (left) and small expansion jaws (right), used for compression mode

EXPANSION JAWS

Expansion jaws can be used to hold the inside of a previously drilled hole, where any potential jaw marks either won't be seen or can be removed at a later stage. Masking tape wrapped around the jaws will reduce marking.

A larger set of expansion jaws

PLASTIC JAWS

Plastic jaws are very useful when holding the spigot to turn the top of the mill. They cause far less indentation on the spigot than metal jaws.

DOVETAIL JAWS

The length of a dovetail tenon can be less than that of a straight tenon, so less additional wood needs to be included on the blank—though this depends on the shape of the very top of the mill. Dovetail jaws of sufficient size will hold a blank well.

SCREW CHUCK

If you plan to drill the 5/16 in. (8 mm) shaft hole in the top of the mill using a drill press before turning, then a suitably sized screw chuck can utilize this hole for holding the top at its spigot end while shaping the outside.

JAM CHUCK

When shaping the mill body, holding the work between a cone-shaped jam chuck in compression jaws and the tailstock is a recommended option.

> **HINTS:**
> If the wood is dark in color, consider using a white pencil to mark the key lines on the blank.
>
> If a large number of mills are to be produced, mark out the key dimensions on a wooden template before transferring them to the individual mill blanks.

MARKING OUT THE BLANK

Usually, I make no more than two or three pairs of mills at any one time, so I simply mark the dimensions on the rough-turned wood with a sharpened pencil, taking care with the accuracy of the measurements.

TURNING THE BLANK

The initial rough turning is carried out in the normal way, between centers and using a roughing gouge, followed by a 1/2 in. (13 mm) beading and parting tool to form the tenons. (I assume that you have allowed extra wood for facing off and for forming the tenon or dovetail, as shown in the example on page 80.) Start turning using a slow speed. When the corners have been removed, the speed can be increased. When the blank is round, stop the lathe and mark out the required tenons or dovetail.

The spigot should be turned to approximately 3/16 in. (5 mm) more than its finished size. The correct diameter can be achieved either by stopping the lathe and checking with preset calipers or, if you feel confident enough, the calipers can be held in one hand over the spigot or tenon while the other hand controls the cut of the parting and beading tool.

Sizing a tenon, using calipers in one hand and a parting and beading tool in the other

DRILLING THE BASE

Most of the drilling required to produce a mill uses sawtooth bits, which cut into endgrain well. It is possible to drill the holes on a drill press; however, there is a risk of the drill wandering if the wood is not held firmly. I suggest that the holes are drilled with the mill on the lathe. The tenon is held in compression jaws, and the sawtooth bit in a Jacobs chuck in the tailstock. When the base is running true, set the lathe to around 800 rpm for drilling.

If you don't have the correct size of sawtooth bit, a smaller one will suffice; the hole can then be opened up using the long point of a ½ in. (13 mm) skew chisel. While drilling, withdraw the bit regularly to release the shavings; this will also reduce the chance of the bit and the wood overheating. The diagrams below and opposite show the drill sizes and depth of cut required for Type 1 and Type 2 mechanisms.

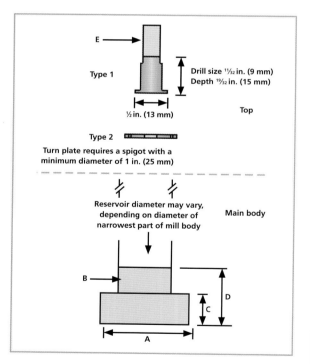

Drill sizes and depths to fit a traditional Type 1 or Type 2 mechanism (See table below for drill sizes)

Boring with a sawtooth bit; remember to withdraw the bit from time to time to prevent overheating and allow shavings to escape

The largest hole is drilled first. The center point for the drill should still be there from roughing out the blank (see top diagram on facing page).

When the base has been drilled, the mill is removed from the lathe and the tenon removed, usually by one of two methods:

1 Using a bandsaw.

2 By securing the inside of the first hole in expansion jaws and bringing the tailstock up, and removing the tenon with a ½ in. (13 mm) spindle gouge or a ⅛ in. (3 mm) parting tool.

If you used the first method, the next stage is to mount the body in either expansion or jumbo jaws. Ensure it is running true, and bring up the tailstock to make a new center point. Face off the body to the right length. Replace the center in the tailstock with the Jacobs chuck and drill the necessary holes to complete the hollowing of the body.

The second method could well leave jaw indentations on the inside of the hole, which may remain visible after the mechanism has been screwed in—but there is usually a chance to remove these marks later.

If you are turning a taller mill, consider buying a sawtooth bit shank extension. This will extend your scope by 6 in. (152 mm) at either end, which makes it possible to design and turn a 20 in. (510 mm) mill.

	A	B	C	D	E
Type 1	1½ in. (38 mm)	¹⁵⁄₁₆ in. (24 mm)	½ in. (13 mm)	Min. 1 in. (25 mm)	¹⁹⁄₆₄ in. (7.5 mm)*
Type 2	1¾ in. (44 mm)	1¹⁄₁₆ in. (27 mm)	½ in. (13 mm)	Min. 1 in. (25 mm)	⁵⁄₁₆ in. (8 mm)

*See opposite page, under "Drilling the top"

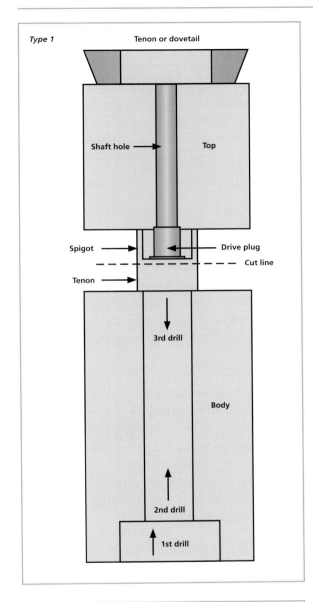

Type 1

Tenon or dovetail

Shaft hole → Top

Spigot → ← Drive plug

----- Cut line

Tenon →

3rd drill

Body

2nd drill

1st drill

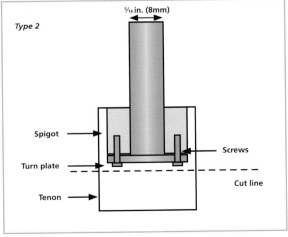

Type 2

⁵⁄₁₆ in. (8mm)

Spigot →

Turn plate →

Screws

----- Cut line

Tenon →

Holes required to fit a traditional mill mechanism

DRILLING THE TOP

Hold the top by its tenon in compression jaws. Ensure that it is running true, and then face off the spigot length to a length of round ⅜ in. (10 mm). Reduce the spigot diameter, using either a ½ in. (13 mm) parting tool or a skew chisel, to a point where it fits easily into the top of the base. An easy fit is one that allows for some movement in the wood, so the top of the mill will still turn if either the spigot or the base becomes slightly oval.

First drill the holes for the Type drive plug as detailed on page 84.

Refer back to the previous page for the drill size for the shaft of the mechanism. It is imperative that the shaft hole is drilled centrally, otherwise the shaft will bind in the top when turned. Just drill the hole halfway through the top at this stage.

Throughout this book I have suggested using a ⁵⁄₁₆ in. (8 mm) drill for the shaft hole, because this is the size recommended by the mechanism manufacturers. In my experience this is too large for a Type 1 mechanism. I would suggest a ¹⁹⁄₆₄ in. (7.5 mm) drill. I accept that this is an odd size, but it works very well.

If you aren't planning to make many mills, then the ⁵⁄₁₆ in. (8 mm) drill will be fine. However, you should consider using a two-part epoxy on the Type 1 drive plug to ensure it stays in place.

When drilling from the top, the spigot can be held in plastic jaws to reduce indentations. When the top is running true, remove the top tenon or dovetail as shown in the diagram and carefully drill the shaft hole to meet the hole drilled earlier.

For a Type 2 mechanism, no additional holes need to be drilled before the shaft hole is drilled. The turn plate's hole positions are marked while holding the turn plate centrally over the shaft hole once the top has been finished and shaped.

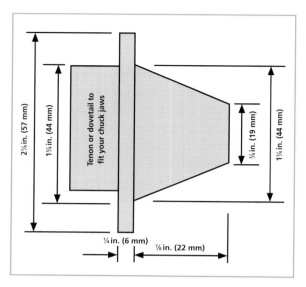

A conical plug to support the mill body while the outside is turned

TURNING THE OUTSIDE OF THE MILL BODY

The body should be held between centers using a cone-shaped plug held in compression jaws, and a cone center in the tailstock.

TURNING THE OUTSIDE OF THE MILL TOP

The important thing here is to limit indentations occurring on the spigot when using metal jaws, given that the spigot has been turned to its finished diameter by now. Plastic jaws do help. Another option is to wrap masking tape evenly around the spigot. Whichever method you use, the blank must be running true before you drill into the top. When drilling is completed, the tailstock can be brought up to keep the blank running true while the outside is shaped.

SANDING

There are many types of sandpaper available; cloth-backed aluminum-oxide paper is my favorite. The tool rest should be removed from the tool rest base and kept out of the way while you sand underneath the wood. Depending on the finish you achieved with your final cuts, begin the sanding phase with 120 grit and move on through 180-, 240-, 320-, and finally 400 grit, which will normally suffice.

The objective of the sanding phase is not only to achieve a smooth finish, but also to remove all signs of sanding, such as lines and uneven sanding marks. You are trying to achieve a smooth finish that leaves only the grain features showing. The speed of the lathe during sanding should be around 500 rpm. Another option, if you are using a lathe with reverse capabilities, is to reverse the sanding direction between grits.

One thing you must try to avoid when sanding is rounding off those sharp corners that give your mill a clean, crisp look. If you created the corners with a skew chisel, you may not need to sand them. After sanding, you can, if necessary, very lightly and carefully touch the edge with a ½ in. (13 mm) skew to bring back the sharpness. Be careful not to slip and either take too much off or chip the edge.

FINISHING

The types of finishes available are detailed on pages 22–25. When you are happy with the sanding process, there are a number of alternative finishes you may wish to apply, such as color, ebonizing, or burning. Whichever finish you choose, you are probably going to need to seal the wood to prevent it from becoming marked or stained during use.

PUTTING THE MILL TOGETHER

Refer back to pages 70–71 to remind yourself of the order of the mechanism components.

DRIVE PLUGS AND PLATES

Depending on which of the two types of traditional mechanism you are planning to use, the plastic drive plugs (Type 1) or the turn plate (Type 2) should be fitted to the spigot. The drill sizes required for the drive plug are detailed on page 84. If you are fitting the turn plate to a salt mill, use stainless-steel screws. The aluminum circular turn plate (Type 2) must be positioned dead center if the sections of the mill are to rotate together evenly. It is important to drill the shaft hole (E) ⁵⁄₁₆ in. (8 mm) in diameter for a Type 2 mechanism.

FITTING THE MECHANISM

Because I turn a large number of mills, I have drilled a ½ in. (13 mm) hole in my bench. Slide the grinding mechanism's individual parts over the shaft in the right order and insert it into the body of the mill. Using an index finger to support the grinding parts, tip the body of the mill over and place the shaft through the hole in the bench. The mechanism retainer can now be positioned over the grinding mechanism, before screwing the retainer into the bottom of the mill's body.

It is worth making pilot holes for the screws. A scriber with a wooden handle can be lightly hammered through one of the retainer's holes at an angle away from the mill's reservoir, to a depth of around ³⁄₁₆ in. (5 mm).

> Remember—the screws used must be:
> - **Salt: stainless steel**
> - **Pepper: zinc-plated steel**
> Salt + ordinary steel = rust!

The first screw can now be loosely fitted, and a pilot hole made for the second screw when you are happy that the mechanism is central in its hole. Fit the second screw and tighten the first. Remove the mill from the bench and screw on the finial nut to ensure that the top can be made tight to the base of the mill. If it doesn't bed down properly, it may be just that the thread of the shaft needs to be filed down a little.

TESTING THE MILL

Before giving the mill to a client I always test it first with either salt or pepper. It is well worth doing this because there is the possibility of something having been put together wrong, and you will sleep better at night knowing that you have produced a quality mill.

Finally, don't forget to tell your client that the top of the mill should only be turned *clockwise*; the mechanism will wear out more quickly if it is turned both ways.

TURNING A PAIR OF MILLS

If you are turning a pair of mills, mark an arrow and a number on each half of each mill using a marker pen. This will make it easier to match the pairs after they have been cut in two and possibly dropped on the floor!

Treat a pair of mills as a production run. If possible, carry out the same operation on both mills using the same chuck jaws. Consider making a template with the shape and dimensions marked on it and using this for marking out the roughed-out blank.

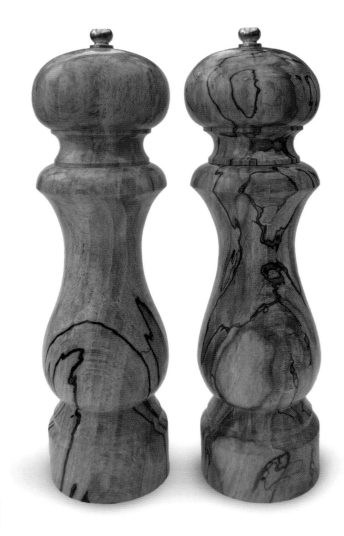

SHORTENING THE SHAFT OF A TYPE 1 MECHANISM

1 Unless you happen to have the appropriate size die, it is easier to shorten the base of the shaft. Loosely assemble the mechanism into the mill with the finial nut screwed to halfway along the thread.

2 Using a sharp pencil, mark a line on the shaft at the point where it meets the base of the grinder.

3 Remove the mechanism and draw a second line ³⁄₁₆ in. (5 mm) nearer to the base end of the shaft. Now saw right through the shaft at this point.

4 Place the shaft in the jaws of a smooth-faced vise and, using a small hacksaw, saw across the corners of the shaft along your remaining pencil line.

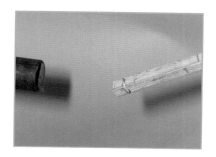

5 Have a piece of a match or a small piece of softwood. Hold the shaft in the vise, protruding about 3 in. (75 mm). Using a propane gas torch, heat the end 1 in. (25 mm) for around 15 seconds. The part of the flame that touches the metal should be just in advance of the inner blue flame. When you dab the softwood on the heated shaft it should smolder and leave a black mark. Success? If so, remove the shaft, taking care not to touch it with your hands. Quench it in either tea, coffee, or water, whichever is the nearest!

6 Now hold the shaft vertically in the vise with your marked ³⁄₁₆ in. (5 mm) protruding and tighten up the vise as much as you can. Take either a tap holder or a mole grip (adjustable spanner), and then tighten it around the end of the shaft. Gently twist the tool a quarter-turn in one direction.

7 The end result should look like this. The bottom of the shaft is now at around 45° to the main shaft. This ensures that the shaft cannot be pulled through the mechanism.

8 Reassemble the mechanism in the mill. With the index finger of one hand pressing against the bottom of the shaft, you should see just enough thread poking from the top to go halfway into the finial nut. OK so far? Next, tighten the finial nut to the point where the top of the mill will not turn; the mechanism can now be screwed into the mill. If the top does still turn when the nut is tightened, then the shaft is still too long.

SHORTENING THE SHAFT OF A TYPE 2 MECHANISM

1 Same as Type 1.

2 Same as Type 1.

3 Mark only ⅛ in. (3 mm) from the first pencil line.

4 Not applicable.

5 Same as Type 1.

6 Not applicable.

7 Not applicable.

8 Using a ball-peen hammer, roll over the edges of the end of the shaft.

9 The end result should look like this.

10 Assemble as described for Type 1 mechanism, step 8.

MILL PROJECTS
(TRADITIONAL MECHANISM)

11 CLASSIC

■ Level of difficulty: **Beginner**

TOOLS

¾ in. (19 mm) spindle roughing gouge
⅜ in. (10 mm) spindle gouge
½ in. (13 mm) spindle gouge
½ in. (13 mm) beading and parting tool
½ in. (13 mm) skew chisel
1 in. (25 mm) skew chisel
½ in. (13 mm) round-nosed scraper
⅛ in. (3 mm) parting tool

Special tools: ½ in. (13 mm) half-round scraper

Mechanism: 10 in. (254 mm) Type 1

WOOD

English oak

Height: 9¾ in. (247 mm)
Diameter: 2⅞ in. (73 mm)
Blank dimensions:
For body and top: 3⅜ x 3⅜ x 12 in.
(85 x 85 x 305 mm)
These dimensions allow for facing off and
for tenons or dovetails that will be removed
as the project proceeds.

The Classic mill is based on traditional mills that are commonly seen; it is probably one of the most popular shapes, and should be in every turner's repertoire.

This mill utilizes all of the features commonly associated with spindle turning and is completed using the two most commonly used tools, the spindle gouge and the skew chisel, to form coves and flat surfaces. The challenge with this mill is careful measurement to ensure that when the two mills are viewed side by side they are an exact matching pair. Finishing is of equal importance: when users run their hands over these pieces they will be looking for a smooth surface and crisp edges. Many of the techniques used in this project will be developed further in the remaining mill projects.

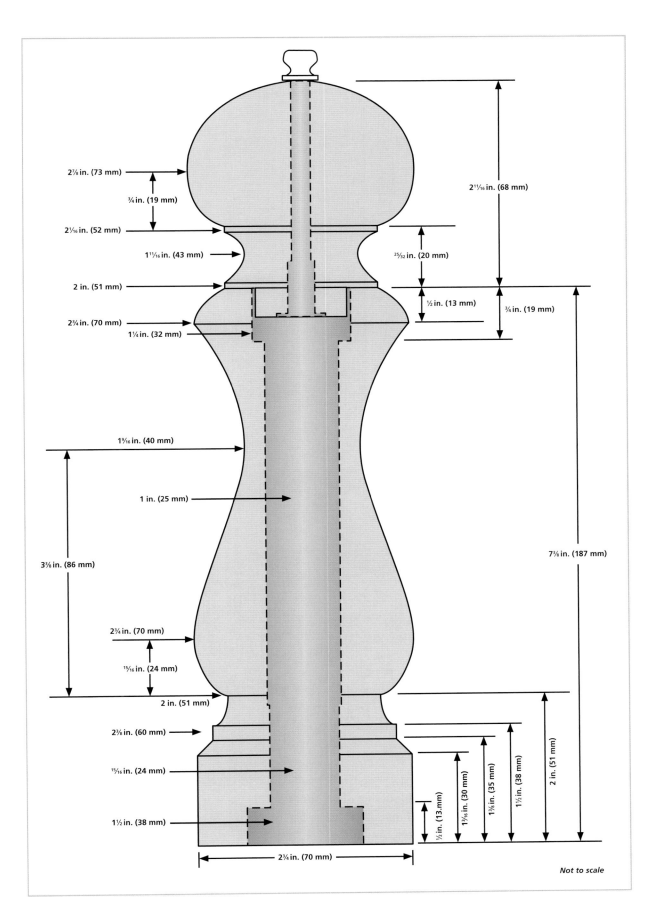

2⅞ in. (73 mm)

¾ in. (19 mm)

2¹/₁₆ in. (52 mm)

1¹¹/₁₆ in. (43 mm)

2 in. (51 mm)

2¾ in. (70 mm)

1¼ in. (32 mm)

1⁹/₁₆ in. (40 mm)

1 in. (25 mm)

3⅜ in. (86 mm)

2¾ in. (70 mm)

¹⁵/₁₆ in. (24 mm)

2 in. (51 mm)

2⅜ in. (60 mm)

¹⁵/₁₆ in. (24 mm)

1½ in. (38 mm)

2¾ in. (70 mm)

2¹¹/₁₆ in. (68 mm)

²⁵/₃₂ in. (20 mm)

½ in. (13 mm)

¾ in. (19 mm)

7⅜ in. (187 mm)

½ in. (13 mm)

1³/₁₆ in. (30 mm)

1⅜ in. (35 mm)

1½ in. (38 mm)

2 in. (51 mm)

Not to scale

BODY

> **HINT:**
> If you are making a pair of mills, mark each half of the mill with a direction line and number. When you have four pieces of wood on your bench you have to be organized, or they easily get mixed up.

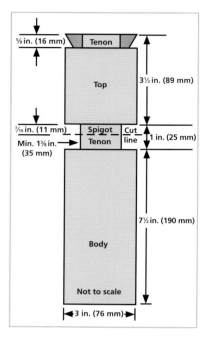

1 Mount the blank between centers and rough-turn to the dimensions shown. Turn the top tenon to a size suitable for your chuck's compression jaws. The middle spigot and tenon should be no less than 1⅜ in. (35 mm) in diameter to allow for any jaw marks to be removed later. Remove the blank from the lathe and bandsaw through at the cut line shown.

> **HINT:**
> If you are planning to turn a pair, you may find it quicker to mount the second blank and repeat steps 2 and 3 before changing your chuck jaws.

2 Mount the body's tenon in compression jaws and ensure that it is running true. Face off the bottom end, making it slightly concave.

The next step is to drill the holes for the mechanism. The first of the recesses requires a 1½ in. (38 mm) diameter hole. Follow this with a ¹⁵⁄₁₆ in. (24 mm) drill to a depth of around 4 in. (102 mm).

3 The tenon at the top end of the body can now be sawn off using a bandsaw. Reverse the blank, holding the base in expansion jaws. Ensure that the body is running true and face off to a length of 7⅜ in. (187 mm). This design requires a 1¼ in. (32 mm) recess to hold the spigot. Remove the tailstock and drill this hole to a depth of ¾ in. (19 mm), then use a 1 in. (25 mm) sawtooth drill to meet the ¹⁵⁄₁₆ in. (24 mm) hole drilled earlier.

4 To turn the outside of the body, it is supported by a cone-shaped jam chuck held in compression jaws in the headstock, and by the tailstock. The dimensions of the jam chuck were given on page 86.

5 With the body mounted between centers as described, turn the straight section at the bottom of the body. Using a ½ in. (13 mm) gouge and a 1 in. (25 mm) skew, reduce the diameter to 2¾ in. (70 mm).

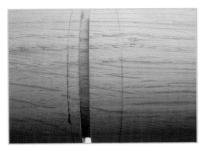

6 Mark out the next three distances from the bottom of the body, as shown in the diagram. Part between the second and third lines with a ⅛ in. (3 mm) parting tool to give a diameter 1/32 in. (1 mm) greater than the finished diameter of 2⅜ in. (60 mm).

7 Chamfer between the first and second lines with a ½ in. (13 mm) skew chisel.

8 Use the long point of the ½ in. (13 mm) skew chisel to mark the transition between the concave and convex curves, as you would when making a bead.

9 Use a ⅜ in. (10 mm) gouge to begin forming the concave shape, but complete it using a ½ in. (13 mm) half-round scraper, as shown.

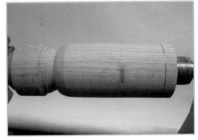

10 Sand from the concave curve to the top of the base, and clean up the flat by touching it lightly with a ⅛ in. (3 mm) parting tool to leave it at the correct diameter and with a sharp edge.

11 Moving to the top end of the mill body, mark a line ½ in. (13 mm) from the end and shape the convex curve using a ½ in. (13 mm) gouge.

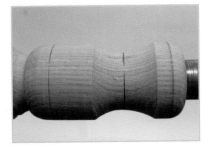

12 Mark the maximum and minimum diameter points along the mill body. Begin to shape the mill to its narrowest diameter using a ½ in. (13 mm) spindle gouge.

  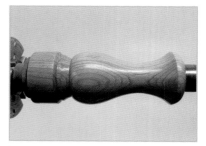

13 Throughout the shaping, keep checking that the narrowest diameter of 1 9/16 in. (40 mm) is at the correct distance of 3 3/8 in. (85 mm) from the bottom, as shown in the measured diagram. This is especially important if you are turning a pair of mills—the eye will pick up any discrepancies in these dimensions.

14 After shaping, sand down through the grits to 400 and seal. With this particular mill I sprayed on a gloss cellulose lacquer. This can be done while the body is still on the lathe. After allowing each coat to dry (this takes around 20 minutes, depending on the temperature), use a white synthetic finishing pad to de-nib the lacquer between coats.

TOP

15 Hold the top by its tenon in either dovetail or compression jaws. Face off the spigot to a length of 3/8 in. (10 mm). Drill using an 11/32 in. (9 mm) bit to a depth of 3/4 in. (19 mm) for the drive plug. Use the 1/2 in. (13 mm) skew to open up this hole to 5/8 in. (16 mm) for a depth of 3/32 in. (2.5 mm) to allow the drive plug to sit flush with the end of the spigot. Complete by drilling the shaft hole to a depth of 2 in. (51 mm).

16 Reduce the spigot diameter to fit into the 1 1/4 in. (32 mm) recess in the top of the mill. The fit should be loose without being sloppy, just enough to prevent any possible future movement of the wood from interfering with the turning action of the mill. Sand and seal the base of the top.

17 The bottom half of the top can now be turned. First, measure the position where the convex curve begins, 25/32 in. (20 mm) from the base. The lower part of the top consists of a concave section with a narrow flat step on either side; note that the upper step is slightly larger in diameter than the lower step. Reduce the flat step nearest to the base to a little over the required 2 in. (51 mm) diameter over a length of 3/8 in. (10 mm). Reduce the diameter adjacent to the convex part to 2 1/16 in. (52 mm).

18 Turn the outside diameter to 3 in. (76 mm). Mark the point of maximum diameter as per the diagram, and begin to turn the convex curve that meets the 2¹⁄₁₆ in. (52 mm) flat step.

19 Turn the concave section using either a ³⁄₈ in. (10 mm) gouge or a ½ in. (13 mm) round-nosed scraper. Sand the curve to 400 grit. Sealing now allows you to see any sanding lines.

20 The top tenon can now be removed, either by using a bandsaw or by reversing the work and holding the bottom spigot in plastic compression jaws. With the tailstock in position, use a ½ in. (13 mm) gouge or a ¹⁄₈ in. (3 mm) parting tool (as shown) to remove most of the tenon, but leave approximately ¹⁄₁₆ in. (1.5 mm) of the tenon in place to allow for any discrepancies in shaping the very top of the mill.

> **HINT:**
> To reduce the risk of marking the spigot with the compression jaws, wrap masking tape around the spigot.

21 The shaft hole should now be drilled through.

22 Begin shaping the top curve. Use a vernier gauge to measure the overall height of the top. To be doubly sure, remove the work from the chuck and, holding a 10 in. (254 mm) mechanism in place, slide the top on and see how much of the threaded shaft is protruding. You should be aiming for around ³⁄₁₆ in. (5 mm).

When you are happy with the shape, sand and seal as you did for the mill body. After spraying and de-nibbing it is advisable to leave the acrylic to harden for 24 hours before buffing with a micro-abrasive polishing compound on a mop and carnauba wax on a separate mop.

The mechanism can now be fitted. First, the drive plug is glued and tapped into place, then the rest of the mechanism is screwed in.

12 MODERN

◾ Level of difficulty: **Beginner**

TOOLS

¾ in. (19 mm) spindle roughing gouge
½ in. (13 mm) spindle gouge
½ in. (13 mm) beading and parting tool
¾ in. (19 mm) skew chisel
¹⁄₁₆ in. (1.5 mm) parting tool
⅛ in. (3 mm) parting tool

Mechanism: 8 in. (203 mm) Type 2

WOOD

Chestnut

Height: 8¼ in. (210 mm)
Diameter: 2⅜ in. (60 mm)
Blank dimensions: 2½ x 2½ x 10⅛ in.
(64 x 64 x 257 mm)

This mill has a very simple shape that lends itself to having the top in a contrasting wood to the body; or the body itself could be ebonized and gilded, as described on page 22—especially if an open-grained wood is chosen.

Mount the blank between centers and rough-turn to the dimensions given. Saw or part as indicated.

BASE

The blank is prepared and drilled as shown on pages 83–85. With the base mounted between a jam chuck and a cone center, rough-turn to a conical shape. Final cuts are made using a ¾ in. (19 mm) skew chisel. After final shaping, sand down through the grits.

TOP

With the top tenon held in compression jaws, face off the spigot to around ³⁄₁₆ in. (5 mm) long. Drill the shaft hole to a depth of 1 in. (25 mm). Now reduce the spigot diameter to fit into the 1¹⁄₁₆ in. (27 mm) hole in the base. This fit should be loose without being sloppy, just enough to allow for any future movement of the wood.

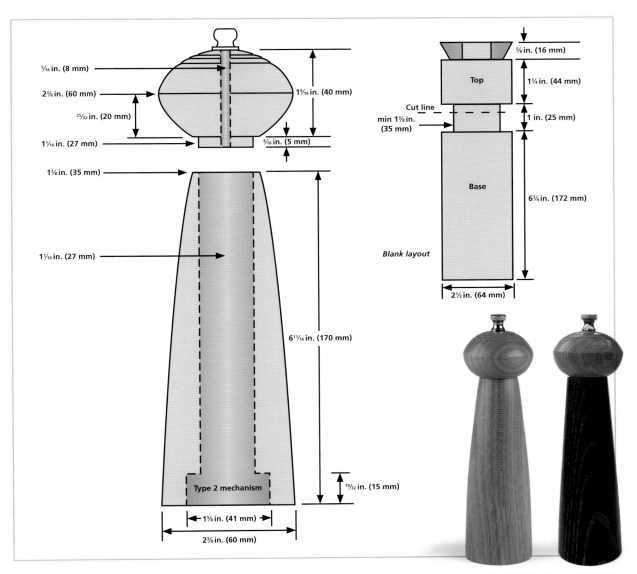

⁵⁄₁₆ in. (8 mm)

2⅜ in. (60 mm)

²⁵⁄₃₂ in. (20 mm)

1¹⁄₁₆ in. (27 mm)

1⅜ in. (35 mm)

1¹⁄₁₆ in. (27 mm)

1⁹⁄₁₆ in. (40 mm)

³⁄₁₆ in. (5 mm)

6¹¹⁄₁₆ in. (170 mm)

Type 2 mechanism

1⅝ in. (41 mm)

2⅜ in. (60 mm)

¹⁹⁄₃₂ in. (15 mm)

⅝ in. (16 mm)

Top

1¾ in. (44 mm)

Cut line

min 1⅜ in. (35 mm)

1 in. (25 mm)

Base

6¾ in. (172 mm)

Blank layout

2½ in. (64 mm)

Hold the spigot in compression jaws and remove the tenon. The shaft hole can now be drilled and the top curved. The three rings on the top can be made using a ¹⁄₁₆ in. (1.5 mm) parting tool, or the long point of a ½ in. (13 mm) skew chisel can be gently pushed in at 90° to the surface—the choice is yours.

Sand and seal as before, and finish with three coats of gloss acrylic lacquer. The Type 2 turn plate and mechanism can now be fitted.

▶ OTHER OPTIONS

If you wish to use a Type 1 mechanism:

• The height of the main body must be reduced to suit the shaft length of the mechanism.

• The appropriate holes for the drive plug and grinding mechanism need to be made.

• Make the reservoir hole ²⁵⁄₃₂ in. (20 mm) diameter.

• The diameter at the top of the main body should be reduced to 1³⁄₁₆ in. (30 mm) and the curve at the base of the top should be adjusted to match this diameter.

13 CAYMAN

TOOLS

¾ in. (19 mm) spindle roughing gouge
⅜ in. (10 mm) spindle gouge
½ in. (13 mm) spindle gouge
½ in. (13 mm) beading and parting tool
½ in. (13 mm) skew chisel
½ in. (13 mm) round-nosed scraper
⅛ in. (3 mm) parting tool

Mechanism: Type 2

WOOD

Chestnut

Height: 4¹¹⁄₃₂ in. (110 mm)
Diameter: 2⅜ in. (60 mm)
Blank dimensions:
For body and top: 2¾ x 2¾ x 5⅝ in.
(70 x 70 x 144 mm)
These dimensions allow for facing off and
for tenons or dovetails that will be removed
as the project proceeds.

This mill was admired by a customer who bought a number of them for his luxury hotel on the Cayman Islands. Naturally, I gave it this name while looking out at the snow and dreaming of beachside restaurants.

This mill involves shortening a mechanism shaft. Rough-turn the blank to the dimensions given.

BODY

Mount the blank's tenon or dovetail in compression jaws and face off the base. Drill the two holes for the mechanism but do not go all the way through with the 1¹⁄₁₆ in. (27 mm) drill.

Part off the body and remove from the lathe. Hold the body's base hole in expansion jaws and finish drilling the 1¹⁄₁₆ in. (27 mm) hole, then face off to the correct length. Remount the body between a cone-shaped jam chuck and a cone center in the tailstock in order to shape the outside.

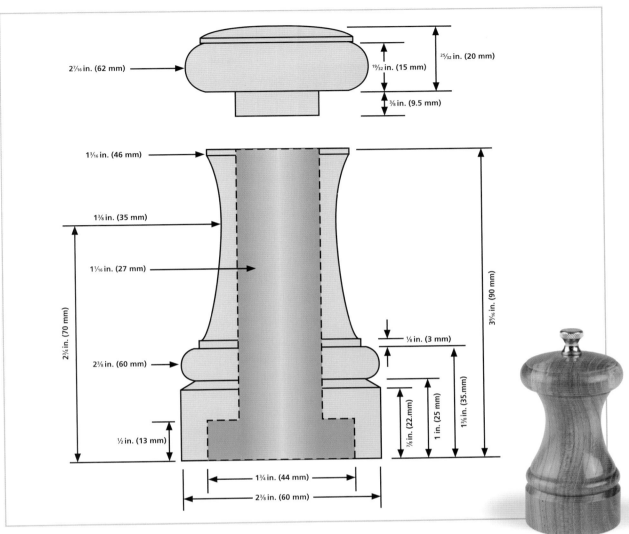

2⁷⁄₁₆ in. (62 mm)

²⁵⁄₃₂ in. (20 mm)

¹⁹⁄₃₂ in. (15 mm)

³⁄₈ in. (9.5 mm)

1³⁄₁₆ in. (46 mm)

1³⁄₈ in. (35 mm)

1¹⁄₁₆ in. (27 mm)

2¾ in. (70 mm)

2³⁄₈ in. (60 mm)

⅛ in. (3 mm)

½ in. (13 mm)

⅞ in. (22 mm)

1 in. (25 mm)

1³⁄₈ in. (35 mm)

3⁹⁄₁₆ in. (90 mm)

1¾ in. (44 mm)

2³⁄₈ in. (60 mm)

TOP

Mount the tenon in compression jaws, ensuring it runs true. Face off the spigot to ⅜ in. (9.5 mm) long, and sand. Partially drill the hole for the shaft. Reduce the spigot diameter to fit in the top of the mill, leaving it just loose enough to allow for possible future movement of the wood. Sand and seal the spigot.

Remove the tenon and remount, holding the bottom spigot in compression jaws. Wrap masking tape round the spigot for protection. When it is running true, drill the shaft hole through and shape the top. Finish the mill using your preferred method. Shorten the shaft (see pages 88–89) and fit the mechanism.

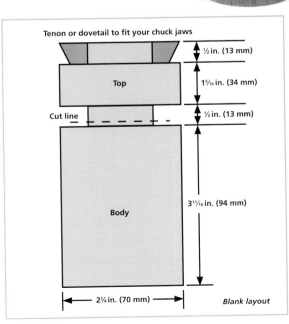

Tenon or dovetail to fit your chuck jaws

½ in. (13 mm)

Top

1⁵⁄₁₆ in. (34 mm)

Cut line

½ in. (13 mm)

Body

3¹¹⁄₁₆ in. (94 mm)

2¾ in. (70 mm)

Blank layout

14 ORIENTAL

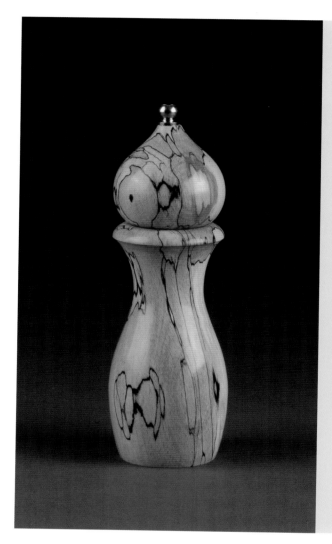

TOOLS

¾ in. (19 mm) spindle roughing gouge
⅜ in. (10 mm) spindle gouge
½ in. (13 mm) spindle gouge
½ in. (13 mm) beading and parting tool
½ in. (13 mm) skew chisel
⅛ in. (3 mm) parting tool

Mechanism: 8 in. (203 mm) Type 1

WOOD

Spalted beech

Height: 7¾ in. (198 mm)
Diameter: 2¹¹⁄₁₆ in. (68 mm)
Blank dimensions: 2⅞ x 2⅞ x 9½ in.
(73 x 73 x 241 mm)
These dimensions allow for facing off and
for tenons or dovetails that will be removed
as the project proceeds.

Mount the blank between centers and rough-turn. Mark off the key lengths and turn the tenons or dovetails. Bandsaw or part as shown in the small diagram opposite.

BASE

Prepare and drill the blank as shown on pages 83–85, and part the top from the base. With the base mounted between a conical jam chuck and a cone center, shape the outside as shown in the main diagram. After final shaping, sand down through the grits to 400, until you are happy that there are no sanding marks, and seal.

TOP

With the top tenon or dovetail in compression jaws, face off the spigot to a length of ⅜ in. (10 mm). Drill the two holes for the drive plug and the shaft hole, as shown on page 85, to a depth of 1 in. (25 mm).

Next, reduce the spigot diameter to fit into the 1 in. (25 mm) hole in the base. This fit should be loose without being sloppy, just enough

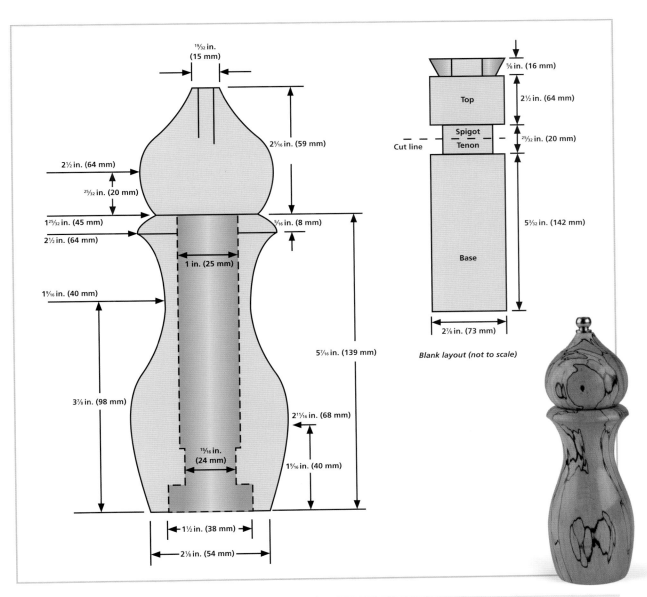

19/32 in. (15 mm)

5/8 in. (16 mm)

2 5/16 in. (59 mm)

Top

2 1/2 in. (64 mm)

2 1/2 in. (64 mm)

Spigot

25/32 in. (20 mm)

25/32 in. (20 mm)

Tenon

Cut line

1 25/32 in. (45 mm)

5/16 in. (8 mm)

2 1/2 in. (64 mm)

1 in. (25 mm)

Base

5 3/32 in. (142 mm)

1 9/16 in. (40 mm)

5 7/16 in. (139 mm)

3 7/8 in. (98 mm)

2 11/16 in. (68 mm)

15/16 in. (24 mm)

1 9/16 in. (40 mm)

2 7/8 in. (73 mm)

Blank layout (not to scale)

1 1/2 in. (38 mm)

2 1/8 in. (54 mm)

to prevent any future movement of the wood interfering with the turning action of the mill. Hold the spigot in compression jaws and remove the tenon. The shaft hole should now be drilled through and the top shaped. Sand and seal.

The Type 1 drive plug and mechanism are now fitted in the usual way. Finish the mill using your preferred method.

▶ **OTHER OPTIONS**

If you wish to fit a Type 2 mechanism, the following changes will be needed:

• The body height should be increased.

• The blank will need to be wider and longer.

• The overall diameter of the base, the wing at the top of the base, and the top itself should be increased by approximately 1/8 in. (3 mm).

• The grinding mechanism hole will need to be resized to fit the mechanism.

15 OLIVE OIL BOTTLE

■ Level of difficulty: **Beginner**

TOOLS
⅜ in. (10 mm) spindle gouge
½ in. (13 mm) spindle gouge
½ in. (13 mm) beading and parting tool
½ in. (13 mm) skew chisel
⅛ in. (3 mm) parting tool

Accessories required: Type 2 slotted-screw finial nut

Mechanism: 8 in. (203 mm) Type 2

WOOD
Spalted beech

Height: 9 in. (229 mm)
Diameter: 2⁹⁄₃₂ in. (58 mm)
Blank dimensions: 2⁹⁄₃₂ x 2⁹⁄₃₂ x 11⅛ in. (58 x 58 x 283 mm)
These dimensions allow for facing off and for tenons or dovetails that will be removed as the project proceeds.

I first saw this shape when I was searching the supermarket shelves for olive oil, and decided that the square shape flowing to the round top would make a distinctive style of mill.

You need access to a thickness planer to get the square section exactly right. This mill uses a slotted-screw finial nut (see pages 74–75). To differentiate between the mills, the words "Salt" and "Pepper" can be engraved on the side (see page 23).

Accurately locate the center of the square blank by using a sharp pencil to mark out the diagonals. Mount the blank between centers and rough-turn. Mark out the key dimensions and turn the tenons or dovetails. Saw or part as shown.

BASE
Prepare and drill the blank is as shown on pages 83–85. With the base mounted between a jam chuck and a cone center, shape the outside according to the diagram.

After final shaping, sand the curved section as normal. For the flat surfaces, use a block of cork with the sandpaper wrapped around it to ensure a smooth, flat surface. The edges are slightly rounded off at this time.

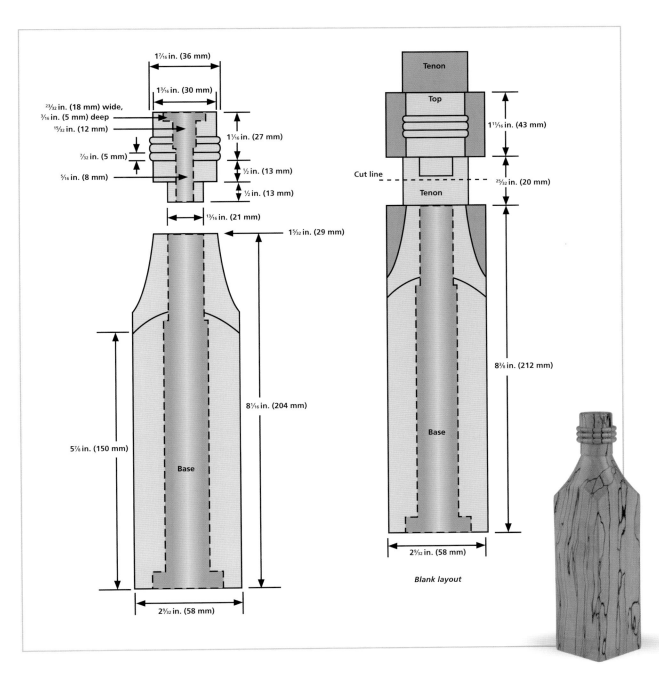

1⁷/₁₆ in. (36 mm)

1³/₁₆ in. (30 mm)

²³/₃₂ in. (18 mm) wide,
³/₁₆ in. (5 mm) deep

¹⁵/₃₂ in. (12 mm)

⁷/₃₂ in. (5 mm)

⁵/₁₆ in. (8 mm)

1¹/₁₆ in. (27 mm)

½ in. (13 mm)

½ in. (13 mm)

¹³/₁₆ in. (21 mm)

1⁵/₃₂ in. (29 mm)

8¹/₁₆ in. (204 mm)

5⁷/₈ in. (150 mm)

Base

2⁹/₃₂ in. (58 mm)

Tenon

Top

1¹¹/₁₆ in. (43 mm)

Cut line

²⁵/₃₂ in. (20 mm)

Tenon

8³/₈ in. (212 mm)

Base

2⁹/₃₂ in. (58 mm)

Blank layout

TOP

With the top tenon in compression jaws, face off the spigot to around ½ in. (13 mm) long. Drill the ⁵/₁₆ in. (8 mm) hole approximately halfway through the top.

Reduce the spigot diameter to fit into the ¹³/₁₆ in. (21 mm) hole in the base. This fit should be loose without being sloppy, just enough to allow for any future movement of the wood.

Hold the spigot in compression jaws and remove the tenon. Drill and open up the hole for the slotted-screw nut to a width of ²³/₃₂ in. (18 mm) and a depth of ³/₁₆ in. (5 mm). Drill a ¹⁵/₃₂ in. (12 mm) hole to a depth of 1 in. (25 mm) and then complete the drilling of the ⁵/₁₆ in. (8 mm) shaft hole. Shape the outside as shown. Sand and seal as usual.

Fit the Type 2 turn plate and mechanism, and finish the mill using your preferred method.

16 CHIANTI BOTTLE

■ Level of difficulty: **Intermediate**

TOOLS
¾ in. (19 mm) spindle roughing gouge
½ in. (13 mm) spindle gouge
½ in. (13 mm) beading and parting tool
½ in. (13 mm) skew chisel
⅛ in. (3 mm) parting tool

Accessories required: Slotted-screw nut

Mechanism: 8 in. (203 mm) Type 1

WOOD
Ash and satiné bloodwood; finial in
pau amarello

Height: 9 in. (230 mm)
Diameter: 3¹⁵/₁₆ in. (100 mm)
Blank dimensions:
Base: 4⅛ x 4⅛ x 4⅜ in. (105 x 105 x 111 mm)
Neck: 3⁹/₁₆ x 3⁹/₁₆ x 4⅛ in. (90 x 90 x 105 mm)
Finial top: 1½ x 1½ x 2¾ in. (38 x 38 x 70 mm)

There are no prizes for guessing what inspired this design. This mill uses a slotted-screw nut, described on pages 74–75. The finial is in a contrasting color to indicate the contents.

BASE
Between centers, rough out and turn the top tenon or dovetail to fit your chuck. Remove from the lathe and hold the tenon in compression jaws. Ensure that it is running true. Face off the bottom of the base. Drill the two holes for the mechanism as described on page 84.

Hold the bottom of the base in expansion jaws. Mark out the length and face off. Drill and open up using a ½ in. (13 mm) skew, the 2⅛ in. (54 mm) reservoir hole to a depth of 1¾ in. (44 mm) and slope this hole to meet the mechanism hole as shown in the main diagram. Turn a recess 3⁵/₁₆ in. (84 mm) wide by ¼ in. (6 mm) deep. Reverse the base, either holding the reservoir end in expansion jaws with tailstock support, or mounting it between centers using a jam chuck. The reason for this? It is easier to turn the bottom bead, away from the chuck jaws. Turn the outside, sand, and seal.

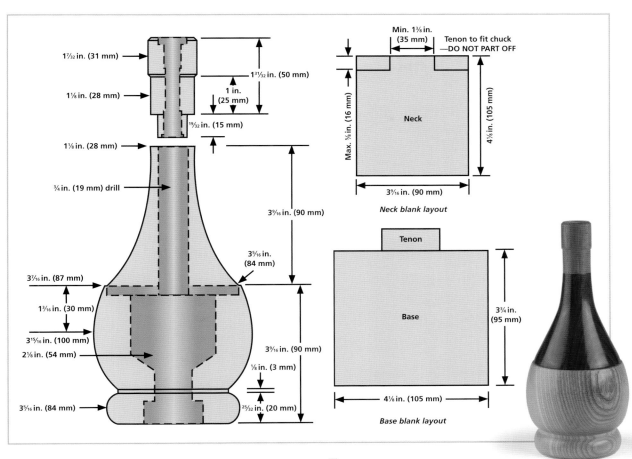

Neck blank layout

Base blank layout

NECK

Between centers, rough out and turn down the top of the neck to a minimum of 1⅜ in. (35 mm) diameter as shown in the small diagram above. Remove from the lathe and mount this tenon in compression jaws. When running true, support with the tailstock and face off the bottom of the neck.

In the base of the neck, drill or turn a hole to fit your expansion jaws. Now drill the reservoir hole to half-depth, using a ¾ in. (19 mm) bit.

Reverse, holding the bottom of the neck in the expansion jaws, face off to 3%16 in. (90 mm), and complete the ¾ in. (19 mm) drilling. The outside of the neck can now be turned, sanded, and sealed, and removed from the lathe.

Remount the base in the expansion jaws and, after aligning the grain of each, glue the neck into the base using PVA glue. Support with the tailstock until dry.

FINIAL

After rough-turning the blank, hold the top half of the finial in compression jaws and form the spigot to fit easily into the top of the mill. The hole for the drive plug is drilled next, followed by the shaft hole for half the distance.

Reverse, holding the work by the spigot, and face off to 1³¹⁄₃₂ in. (50 mm) before drilling the holes for the slotted-screw nut and completing the drilling of the shaft hole. Shape the outside, sand, and seal.

The Type 1 drive plug and mechanism can now be fitted.

▶ **OTHER OPTIONS**

If you wish to fit a Type 2 mechanism, the height of the body and neck should be increased by the appropriate amount.

17 ELIZABETHAN

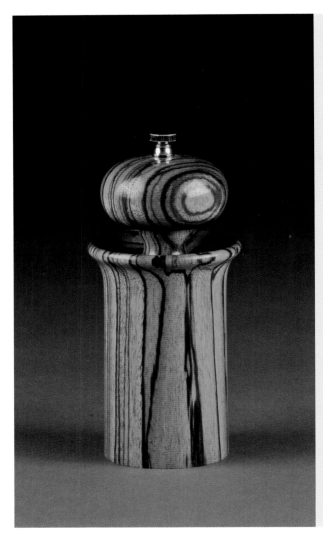

■ Level of difficulty: **Intermediate**

TOOLS

¾ in. (19 mm) spindle roughing gouge
⅜ in. (10 mm) spindle gouge
½ in. (13 mm) spindle gouge
½ in. (13 mm) beading and parting tool
½ in. (13 mm) round-nosed scraper
½ in. (13 mm) skew chisel
⅛ in. (3 mm) parting tool

Accessories required: None

Mechanism: 6 in. (152 mm) Type 2

WOOD

Zebrano

Height: 6 in. (152 mm)
Diameter: 3 in. (76 mm)
Blank dimensions: 3⅛ x 3⅛ wx 8¾ in.
(79 x 79 x 222 mm)
These dimensions allow for facing off and
for tenons or dovetails that will be removed
as the project proceeds.

This mill has a flared collar around the top of the body, which reminded me of an
Elizabethan courtier's neck ruff.

Mount the blank between centers, mark out
the key dimensions, rough out, and part the
two halves.

BASE

Hold the tenon of the base in compression jaws
and ensure that it is running true. Face off the
bottom and sand. The 1¾ in. (44 mm) hole for
the grinding mechanism is drilled first, followed
by the 1¹⁄₁₆ in. (27 mm) hole to a depth of around
2¾ in. (70 mm).

Reverse the base, holding in expansion jaws;
when it is running true, support the work with
the tailstock to allow the tenon to be removed
and the base to be faced off to the correct
length. The 1¼ in. (32 mm) hole is drilled to
a depth of ⁵⁄₃₂ in. (4 mm), followed by a 1 in.
(25 mm) hole to meet the existing 1¹⁄₁₆ in.
(27 mm) hole. Then, shape the top of the base
using a ½ in. (13 mm) round-nosed scraper and
a ½ in. (13 mm) spindle gouge.

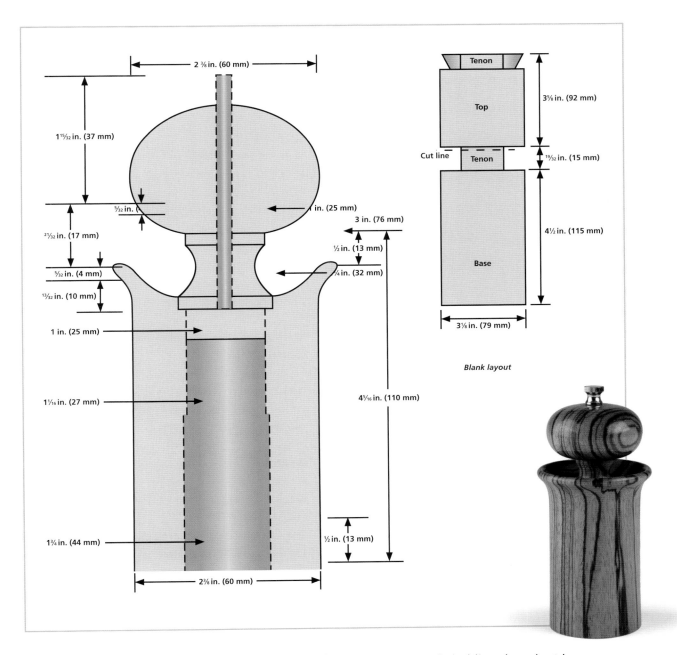

2 ⅜ in. (60 mm)

1¹⁵⁄₃₂ in. (37 mm)

⁵⁄₃₂ in. ( )

in. (25 mm)

2¹⁄₃₂ in. (17 mm)

⁵⁄₃₂ in. (4 mm)

1³⁄₃₂ in. (10 mm)

1 in. (25 mm)

1¹⁄₁₆ in. (27 mm)

1¾ in. (44 mm)

2⅜ in. (60 mm)

3 in. (76 mm)

½ in. (13 mm)

¼ in. (32 mm)

4⁵⁄₁₆ in. (110 mm)

½ in. (13 mm)

Tenon

Top

3⅝ in. (92 mm)

Cut line

Tenon

1⁹⁄₃₂ in. (15 mm)

Base

4½ in. (115 mm)

3⅛ in. (79 mm)

Blank layout

Mount the base between a jam chuck and a cone center to shape the cylindrical part to its final diameter of 2⅜ in. (60 mm). After final shaping, sand down through the grits to 400.

TOP

With the top tenon in compression jaws, turn the overall diameter to just over the required 2⅜ in. (60 mm). Drill the hole for the shaft to a depth of around ⅞ in. (22 mm). Turn the spigot to a length of around ¹³⁄₃₂ in. (10 mm). Shape the bottom half of the top, sand, and seal.

Reverse the work, holding the spigot in compression jaws. Remove the tenon when it is running true. The shaft hole is now drilled through and the rest of the top shaped. Sand and seal the top.

My mill was treated with finishing oil and de-nibbed between coats before finally being power-buffed.

Finally, fit the Type 2 turn plate and mechanism.

18 SPHERICAL COMBO

TOOLS

¾ in. (19 mm) spindle roughing gouge
⅜ in. (10 mm) spindle gouge
½ in. (13 mm) spindle gouge
½ in. (13 mm) beading and parting tool
½ in. (13 mm) skew chisel
⅛ in. (3 mm) parting tool
⅜ in. (10 mm) square-ended scraper
1⅞ in. (47 mm) radius template, made from plastic or any hard material

Mechanism: 4 in. (102 mm) Type 1 with shortened shaft

WOOD

English walnut, with a contrasting wood for the salt top. Masur birch was used here.

Height: 3⁵⁄₁₆ in. (84 mm)
Diameter: 3¹¹⁄₁₆ in. (94 mm)
Blank dimensions: 4 x 4 x 5¼ in. (100 x 100 x 133 mm).
These dimensions allow for facing off and for tenons or dovetails that will be removed as the project proceeds.

A combo is a combined pepper mill and salt shaker. The idea for this one came from a spherical candle. A decorative groove enlivens the simple shape.

Mount the blank between centers and rough-turn. Mark out the key dimensions and turn the tenons and spigot (see diagram, bottom page 111). Part off or bandsaw into two.

BODY

Holding the tenon in compression jaws, face off. Drill using a suitably sized Forstner bit to a depth of 1 in. (25 mm). Open this hole to 2⅜ in. (60 mm). Reverse, and, using either a jam chuck or suitable expansion jaws, remove the tenon and face off to 2 in. (51 mm) long. Drill the two holes required for the pepper-grinding mechanism.

TOP, FIRST STAGE

Holding the tenon in compression jaws, face off the spigot to ³⁄₁₆ in. (5 mm) long. Drill the holes for the drive plug and the shaft clearance hole to around ¾ in. (19 mm) deep. Reduce the spigot to a tight fit to the body. Reverse the top and hold the spigot in compression jaws with masking tape wrapped round it. Drill the shaft clearance hole.

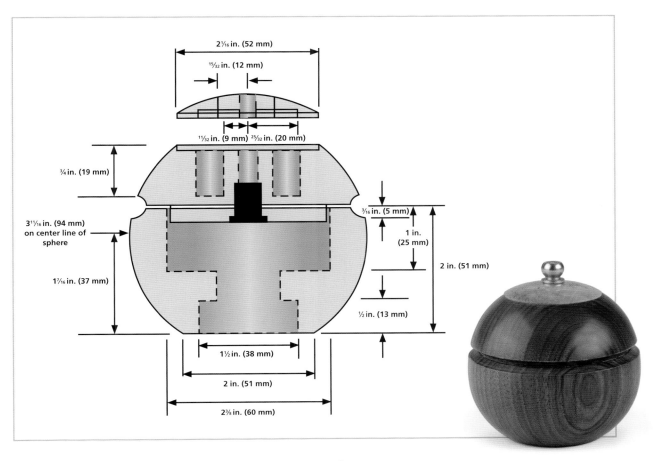

2¹/₁₆ in. (52 mm)

¹⁵/₃₂ in. (12 mm)

¹¹/₃₂ in. (9 mm) ²⁵/₃₂ in. (20 mm)

¾ in. (19 mm)

3¹¹/₁₆ in. (94 mm) on center line of sphere

1⁷/₁₆ in. (37 mm)

³/₁₆ in. (5 mm)

1 in. (25 mm)

2 in. (51 mm)

½ in. (13 mm)

1½ in. (38 mm)

2 in. (51 mm)

2⅜ in. (60 mm)

SHAPING THE OUTSIDE

Push the body and top together and support them between a conical jam chuck and the tailstock. To turn an accurate sphere, make a semicircular template with a radius of 1⅞ in. (47 mm). Carefully turn the mill to a sphere, checking regularly for accuracy. Use a ⅜ in. (10 mm) spindle gouge to turn the groove between the halves. Sand and seal.

TOP, FINAL STAGE

Hold the spigot in compression jaws as before and carefully hollow out the ring-shaped salt reservoir.

SALT CAP INSERT

From a contrasting piece of wood, turn a cylinder to fit into the top of the salt-reservoir hole. While it is still a cylinder, drill the salt holes and the hole for the mill's shaft. Re-hold the top's spigot as before. Insert the salt cap with support from the tailstock and shape it as shown.

ASSEMBLY

Hold the body in expansion jaws by means of the 1½ in. (38 mm) hole for the grinding mechanism. When it is running true, relieve the 2⅜ in. (60 mm) hole sufficiently for the spigot to rotate freely.

Shorten the shaft of the mechanism as described on pages 88–89. Fit the drive plug and mechanism to complete the combo mill.

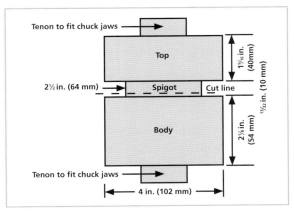

Tenon to fit chuck jaws

Top

1⁹/₁₆ in. (40mm)

2½ in. (64 mm)   Spigot   Cut line

¹³/₃₂ in. (10 mm)

Body

2⅛ in. (54 mm)

Tenon to fit chuck jaws

4 in. (102 mm)

Blank layout

19 VINEGAR BOTTLE (VERSION 1)

TOOLS

¾ in. (19 mm) spindle roughing gouge
⅜ in. (10 mm) spindle gouge
½ in. (13 mm) spindle gouge
½ in. (13 mm) beading and parting tool
½ in. (13 mm) skew chisel
⅛ in. (3 mm) parting tool

Accessories required: ³⁄₁₆ in. (5 mm) insert nut

Mechanism: 8 in. (203 mm) Type 1

WOOD

Olive and cocobolo

Height: 7⅜ in. (187 mm)
Diameter: 2⅞ in. (73 mm)
Blank dimensions:
Body: 3⅛ x 3⅛ x 6⅜ in. (80 x 80 x 162 mm)
Top: 2¾ x 2¾ x 4 in. (70 x 70 x 102 mm)
Finial: 2⅜ x 2⅜ x 2¼ in. (60 x 60 x 57 mm)

The Vinegar Bottle mill was inspired by a pottery vinegar bottle made by Bryan Newman, a wonderful potter from Allar in Somerset, England. I describe two variations, both the same shape but with different grinding mechanisms.

HOLLOWING THE BODY

Rough-turn the blank for the mill body between centers. Mount it by the tenon in compression jaws and face off the base before drilling the 1½ in. (38 mm) and ¹⁵⁄₁₆ in. (24 mm) holes as shown in the diagram of the body blank.

Reverse the blank and hold in expansion mode. Ensure the base is running true, or you will have problems later with a lack of concentricity. Face off to the correct length and drill the 1 in. (25 mm) hole to meet the ¹⁵⁄₁₆ in. (24 mm) hole.

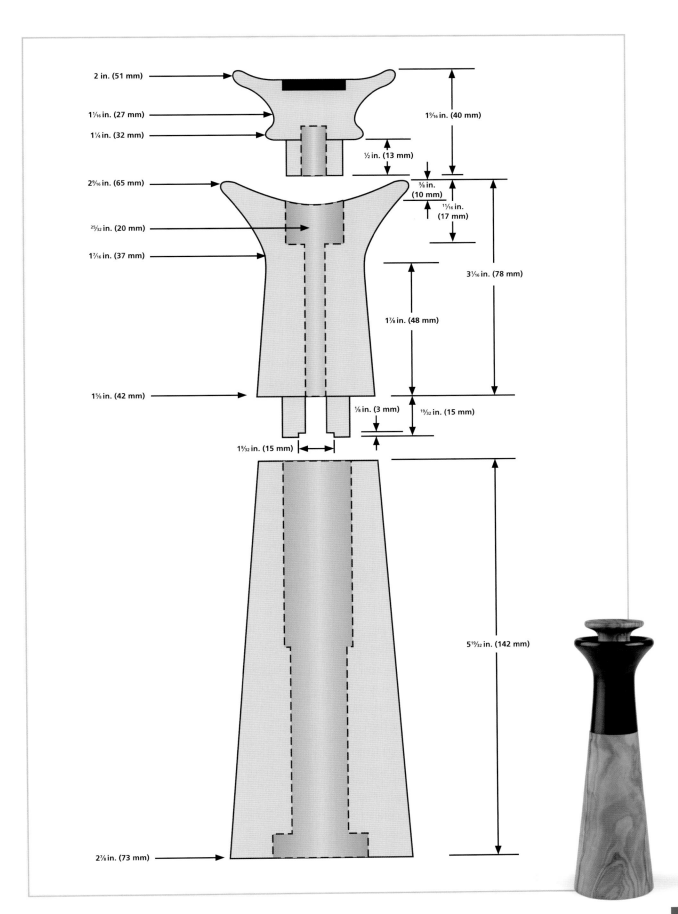

2 in. (51 mm)

1¹⁄₁₆ in. (27 mm)

1¼ in. (32 mm)

1⁹⁄₁₆ in. (40 mm)

½ in. (13 mm)

2⁹⁄₁₆ in. (65 mm)

⅜ in. (10 mm)

¹¹⁄₁₆ in. (17 mm)

²⁵⁄₃₂ in. (20 mm)

1⁷⁄₁₆ in. (37 mm)

3¹⁄₁₆ in. (78 mm)

1⅞ in. (48 mm)

1⅝ in. (42 mm)

⅛ in. (3 mm)

¹⁹⁄₃₂ in. (15 mm)

1⁹⁄₃₂ in. (15 mm)

5¹⁹⁄₃₂ in. (142 mm)

2⅞ in. (73 mm)

FITTING THE TOP TO THE BODY

Drill the holes for the drive plug and shaft, as shown in the diagram of the top blank. The 9/32 in. (7.5 mm) hole should only be drilled halfway. Then turn the spigot. It is essential to make this a tight fit into the base at this stage. If you do take too much off the spigot diameter, wrap masking tape carefully around it until the fit is tight. The holes for the shaft and the finial nut will be drilled later.

SHAPING THE OUTSIDE

The base and the top of the mill need to be pushed together for this phase. There are two choices for holding the two parts between centers:

1 Expansion jaws could be used to hold the bottom of the mill, with support from the tailstock. The disadvantage of this method is that the jaws can mark the wood.

2 A jam-fit chuck solves the marking problem. This is shown on page 86.

Fit the parts together and, when both are running true, turn the straight parts of the base and the top.

DRILLING AND SHAPING THE TOP

It is easier to turn the outside sweeping curve and the very top of the mill after the two sections have been separated. This allows the top of the mill to be turned at a shorter distance from the headstock. Hold the tenon of the top of the mill in compression jaws, supported by the tailstock. Reduce the diameter of the spigot until you have a fit that allows the top to turn freely without being sloppy.

Reverse the work, holding the spigot in expansion jaws. Remove the tenon and complete the final concave shaping. Drill a 25/32 in. (20 mm) hole to a depth of 11/16 in. (17 mm). Complete the hole for the shaft using the 9/32 in. (7.5 mm) drill.

DRILLING THE FINIAL BLANK

Rough down the finial blank between centers and, using compression jaws to hold the top tenon, turn the spigot to ¾ in. (19 mm) diameter for a length of ½ in. (13 mm). Drill the hole for the insert nut to a depth of 19/32 in. (15 mm). You will need to check the dimensions of your insert nut to be sure that the hole you drill is sufficiently large to avoid splitting the wood when you insert the nut.

Holding the spigot in compression jaws, remove the tenon. The finial nut can now be shaped. If you wish, a 1 in. (25 mm) hole can be drilled in the top for a depth of 3/16 in. (5 mm) to allow an identification plug to be turned and inserted.

Although the insert nut may well remain secure by just being tapped in, I always add a two-part epoxy adhesive to make sure.

FITTING THE TYPE 1 MECHANISM

I recommend applying two-part epoxy adhesive to the drive plug before tapping it into the spigot. Assemble the mechanism with the shaft through it. Screw on the finial. If all is well, when the finial nut is fully tightened, the two halves of the mill will be tight. The mechanism can now be screwed in.

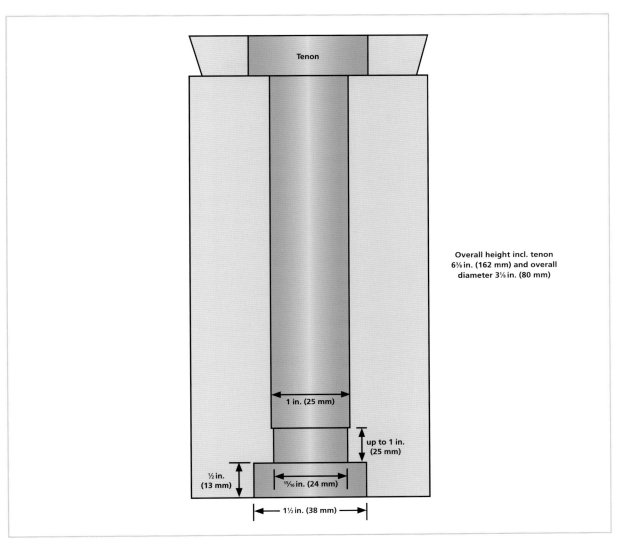

Tenon

Overall height incl. tenon
6⅜ in. (162 mm) and overall
diameter 3⅛ in. (80 mm)

1 in. (25 mm)

up to 1 in.
(25 mm)

½ in.
(13 mm)

¹⁵⁄₁₆ in. (24 mm)

1½ in. (38 mm)

Blank dimensions for Type 1 mill body

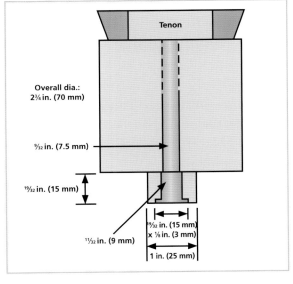

Tenon

Overall dia.:
2¾ in. (70 mm)

⁵⁄₃₂ in. (7.5 mm)

¹⁹⁄₃₂ in. (15 mm)

¹⁵⁄₃₂ in. (15 mm)
x ⅛ in. (3 mm)

¹¹⁄₃₂ in. (9 mm)

1 in. (25 mm)

Blank dimensions for Type 1 top

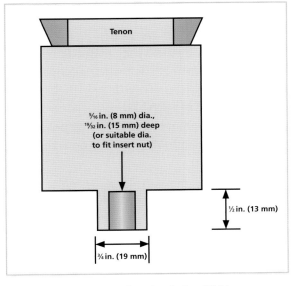

Tenon

⁵⁄₁₆ in. (8 mm) dia.,
¹⁹⁄₃₂ in. (15 mm) deep
(or suitable dia.
to fit insert nut)

½ in. (13 mm)

¾ in. (19 mm)

Blank dimensions for Type 1 finial

VINEGAR BOTTLE (VERSION 2)

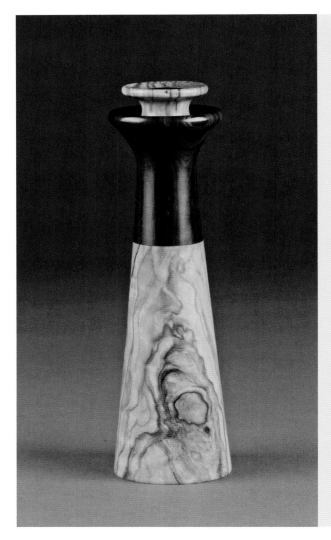

Level of difficulty: **Intermediate**

TOOLS
Same as Version 1, page 112, plus:
Recess tool

Mechanism: 8 in. (203 mm) CrushGrind® shaft

WOOD
Olive and cocobolo

Height: 7⅜ in. (187 mm)
Diameter: 2⅞ in. (73 mm)
Blank dimensions: As Version 1

This version of the Vinegar Bottle has been adapted to use a CrushGrind® shaft mechanism. The finial in this case is for decoration only.

DRILLING THE BASE
Refer to the diagram opposite for the hole diameters and depths required for both the base and the top.

Mount the base between centers and turn a tenon or dovetail to fit your chuck's compression jaws. Remount the base in your chuck and ensure that it is running true. Trim to a length of 5¹⁹⁄₃₂ in. (142 mm) and true up both faces to ensure they are square. Then drill the necessary holes using the process that is described in more detail on pages 132–134.

DRILLING THE TOP
Mount the blank between centers, rough out and true up the length to 4¹⁄₁₆ in. (103 mm). This allows for the 1 in. (25 mm) tenon, which can now be turned down until it is a tight fit into the top of the main body. Drill and make the recess to the dimensions shown opposite.

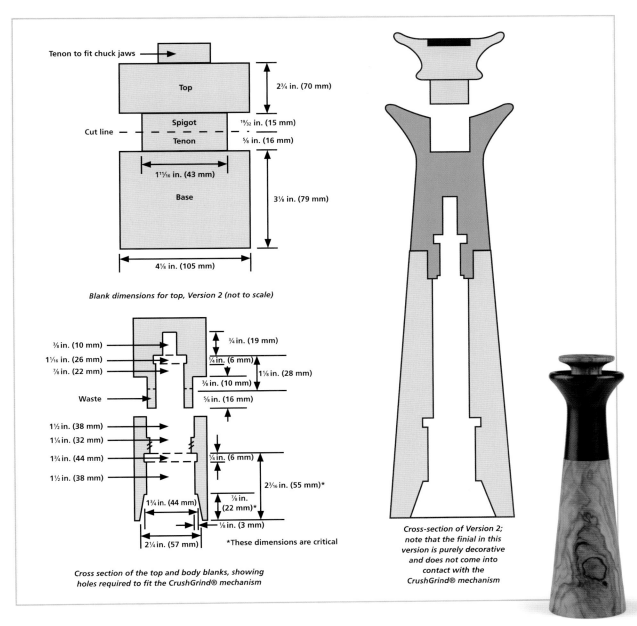

Tenon to fit chuck jaws

Top

2¾ in. (70 mm)

Spigot — 19/32 in. (15 mm)

Cut line

Tenon — ⅝ in. (16 mm)

1¹¹/₁₆ in. (43 mm)

Base

3⅛ in. (79 mm)

4⅛ in. (105 mm)

Blank dimensions for top, Version 2 (not to scale)

⅜ in. (10 mm)
1¹/₁₆ in. (26 mm)
⅞ in. (22 mm)

Waste

¾ in. (19 mm)
¼ in. (6 mm)
1⅛ in. (28 mm)
⅜ in. (10 mm)
⅝ in. (16 mm)

1½ in. (38 mm)
1¼ in. (32 mm)
1¾ in. (44 mm)
1½ in. (38 mm)

¼ in. (6 mm)
2³/₁₆ in. (55 mm)*
⅞ in. (22 mm)*

1¾ in. (44 mm)
⅛ in. (3 mm)

2¼ in. (57 mm)

*These dimensions are critical

Cross section of the top and body blanks, showing holes required to fit the CrushGrind® mechanism

Cross-section of Version 2; note that the finial in this version is purely decorative and does not come into contact with the CrushGrind® mechanism

SHAPING THE BODY

This is done in the same way as for Version 1. The only difference is that the bottom hole of the main body needs to be widened to give better access to the adjusting nut. Hold by its tenon and refer to the cross-section diagram above for the dimensions. The two parts can now be finished as required.

MAKING THE FINIAL

There is no drilling involved in turning the finial nut. Refer to the diagram of Version 1 for the blank size and finished dimensions. The spigot only needs to be ⅜ in. (10 mm) long. As with Version 1, hold the spigot in compression jaws and remove the tenon. The finial can now be shaped. If you wish, a 1 in. (25 mm) hole can be drilled in the top for a depth of ³/₁₆ in. (5 mm) to allow an identification plug to be turned and inserted. The final stage of construction is to glue this into the top of the mill.

COMPLETION

Refer to page 137 for advice on how to fit the mechanism. The mill can now be finished as required.

20 Armless man

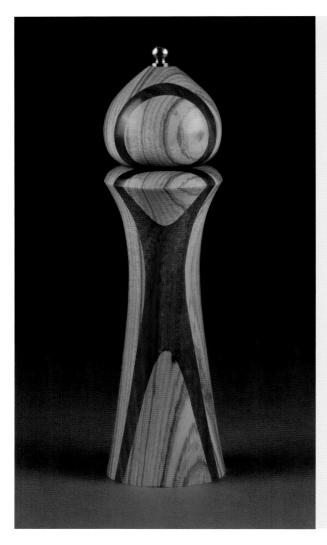

Tools
¾ in. (19 mm) spindle roughing gouge
¼ in. (6 mm) spindle gouge
⅜ in. (10 mm) spindle gouge
½ in. (13 mm) spindle gouge
½ in. (13 mm) beading and parting tool
⅛ in. (3 mm) parting tool

Mechanism: 10 in. (255 mm) Type 1

Wood
Beli and bloodwood

Height: 10 in. (255 mm)
Diameter: 2¾ in. (70 mm)
Blank dimensions: Beli, 2¼ x 3⅛ x 11⅞ in.
(57 x 79 x 302 mm)
Beli, ⅝ x 3⅛ x 11⅞ in. (16 x 79 x 302 mm)
Bloodwood, ¼ x 3⅛ x 11⅞ in. (6 x 79 x 302 mm)
These dimensions include sufficient wood for
facing off and for tenons or dovetails that will
be removed as the project proceeds.

This project uses off-center lamination to create a striking human-like figure from two contrasting woods. You may wish to try different combinations on scrap pieces of wood to achieve an interesting shape of your own. Access to a thickness planer is required.

The two pieces of beli are planed on one side, and the bloodwood on both sides. Glue and clamp the three pieces together. When fully set, mount the blank between centers and rough-turn. Mark the key distances and turn the tenons or dovetails and the spigot. Saw or part as shown.

Base
Prepare and drill the blank as shown earlier. With the base mounted between a jam chuck and a cone center, shape the outside. After final shaping, sand down through the grits to 400, until there are no sanding marks.

Top
With the top tenon in compression jaws, face off the spigot to around ⅜ in. (9.5 mm) in length. Drill the two holes for the drive plug and the shaft hole, as shown on page 85. The shaft hole should be to a depth of approximately

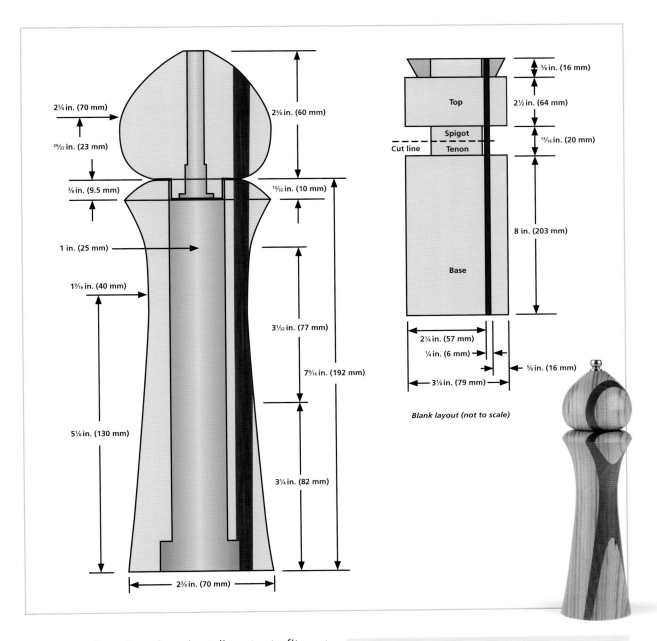

2¾ in. (70 mm)

²⁹/₃₂ in. (23 mm)

2⅜ in. (60 mm)

⅜ in. (9.5 mm)

¹³/₃₂ in. (10 mm)

1 in. (25 mm)

1⁹/₁₆ in. (40 mm)

3¹/₃₂ in. (77 mm)

7⁹/₁₆ in. (192 mm)

5⅛ in. (130 mm)

3¼ in. (82 mm)

2¾ in. (70 mm)

⅝ in. (16 mm)

Top

2½ in. (64 mm)

Spigot

¹³/₁₆ in. (20 mm)

Cut line   Tenon

8 in. (203 mm)

Base

2¼ in. (57 mm)

¼ in. (6 mm)

⅝ in. (16 mm)

3⅛ in. (79 mm)

Blank layout (not to scale)

1 in. (25 mm). Reduce the spigot diameter to fit into the 1 in. (25 mm) hole in the base. This fit should be just loose enough to allow for any possible future movement of the wood. Hold the spigot in compression jaws and remove the tenon. The shaft hole should now be drilled through and the top shaped.

Sand, seal, and finish as desired. The Type 1 drive plug and mechanism can now be fitted.

▶ OTHER OPTIONS

If you wish to fit a Type 2 mechanism, the following changes will need to be made:

• The body's height should be increased.

• The overall diameter of the base and the top should be increased by around ⅛ in. (3 mm).

• The grinding mechanism's hole will be a different diameter.

21 FINLANDIA

■ Level of difficulty: **Intermediate**

TOOLS

¾ in. (19 mm) spindle roughing gouge
½ in. (13 mm) spindle gouge
½ in. (13 mm) beading and parting tool
¾ in. (19 mm) skew chisel
¹⁄₁₆ in. (1.5 mm) parting tool
⅛ in. (3 mm) parting tool

Mechanism: 8 in. (203 mm) Type 1

WOOD

Cherry; walnut or wengé finial

Height: 8 in. (203 mm)
Diameter: 2⁹⁄₁₆ in. (65 mm)
Blank dimensions:
Body: 8⅝ x 2¾ x 2¾ in. (220 x 70 x 70 mm)
Finial 1 (walnut): upright, 1¼ x 1¼ x 2½ in.
(32 x 32 x 64 mm); crosspiece, ⁷⁄₁₆ x ⁷⁄₁₆ x 3 in.
(11 x 11 x 76 mm); brass pin
Finial 2 (wengé): upright, 2½ x 2½ x 1¼ in.
(63.5 x 63.5 x 32 mm); crosspiece, 1 x ²¹⁄₃₂ x
2⁹⁄₁₆ in. (25 x 16.5 x 65 mm); brass pin

This project is all about finials. Each of the alternative finial designs incorporates an M5 threaded insert nut that screws onto the top of the mechanism shaft. The shape of the mill itself is very simple.

Mount the blank between centers and rough-turn. Mark the key dimensions and turn the tenons or dovetails. Saw or part off as shown.

BASE

Prepare and drill the blank in the usual way. With the work mounted between a jam chuck and a cone center, rough-turn to a conical shape, then remove from the lathe.

TOP

With the top tenon held in compression jaws, face off the spigot to around ⅜ in. (10 mm) long. Drill the holes for the drive plug and the shaft hole to a depth of 1 in. (25 mm). Reduce the spigot diameter to fit reasonably tightly in the 1 in. (25 mm) hole in the base. (The fit will be eased after the outside turning of the top and base are completed.)

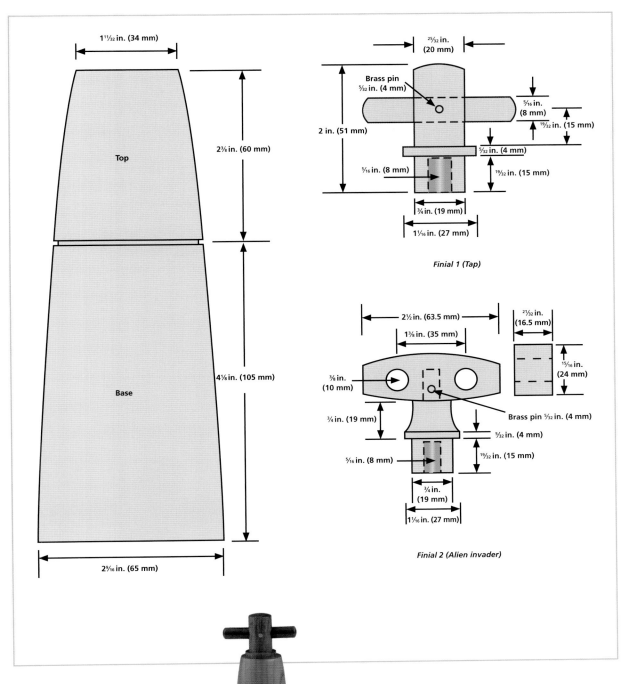

Top

1¹¹⁄₃₂ in. (34 mm)

2³⁄₈ in. (60 mm)

Base

4⅛ in. (105 mm)

2⁹⁄₁₆ in. (65 mm)

25⁄₃₂ in. (20 mm)

Brass pin 5⁄₃₂ in. (4 mm)

2 in. (51 mm)

5⁄₁₆ in. (8 mm)

19⁄₃₂ in. (15 mm)

5⁄₃₂ in. (4 mm)

5⁄₁₆ in. (8 mm)

19⁄₃₂ in. (15 mm)

¾ in. (19 mm)

1¹⁄₁₆ in. (27 mm)

Finial 1 (Tap)

2½ in. (63.5 mm)

1³⁄₈ in. (35 mm)

2¹⁄₃₂ in. (16.5 mm)

15⁄₁₆ in. (24 mm)

⅜ in. (10 mm)

Brass pin 5⁄₃₂ in. (4 mm)

¾ in. (19 mm)

5⁄₃₂ in. (4 mm)

5⁄₁₆ in. (8 mm)

19⁄₃₂ in. (15 mm)

¾ in. (19 mm)

1¹⁄₁₆ in. (27 mm)

Finial 2 (Alien invader)

Hold the spigot in compression jaws and remove the tenon. Drill using a ²⁵⁄₃₂ in. (20 mm) drill to a depth of ²⁵⁄₃₂ in. (20 mm). The shaft hole can now be drilled through.

TURNING THE OUTSIDE

With the top and base pushed together between a conical jam chuck and the cone center, complete the outside using a ¾ in. (19 mm) skew chisel. After final shaping, sand through the grits to 400, until there are no sanding marks. Finally, holding the top between a jam chuck and the cone center, reduce the spigot to fit into the base.

FINIAL 1 (TAP)

Take your square blank of walnut for the upright, mark the hole for the crosspiece, and drill. Mount between centers and turn to 1¹⁄₁₆ in. (27 mm) diameter. Remount the top end in compression jaws. When running true, turn the spigot to its correct diameter and length. Drill a hole for the threaded insert nut, as described on page 76. Remove from the lathe. This is a good time to glue and knock in the insert nut. The spigot is now held in suitable jaws and the top half shaped.

The horizontal crosspiece is turned and glued centrally into the main body of the finial. To give a more secure fixing, I drilled through both pieces to take a length of ⁵⁄₃₂ in. (4 mm) brass rod.

The Tap finial was sealed, sprayed with acrylic lacquer, and finally buffed using White Diamond and wax.

FINIAL 2 (ALIEN INVADER)

The upright part is turned in a very similar way to Finial 1. The top end is turned into a ⁵⁄₁₆ in. (8 mm) dowel, into which the horizontal crosspiece is glued and pinned.

The crosspiece is not turned. The blank is planed with 90° sides to a size slightly larger than the finished item. On one face, mark out and drill the two ³⁄₈ in. (10 mm) holes. Transfer a center line round to one side and mark the position for the ⁵⁄₁₆ in. (8 mm) dowel that you turned earlier. The curved sides can be shaped on a table sanding disk. The Alien finial was finished the same way as the Tap.

The completed Alien Invader mill is shown on page 76.

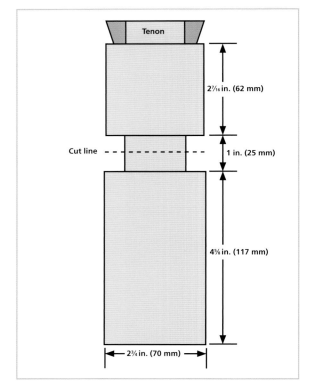

Layout of mill body blank

Finial 1 (Tap)

Finial 2 (Alien invader)

22 THREE-SIDED

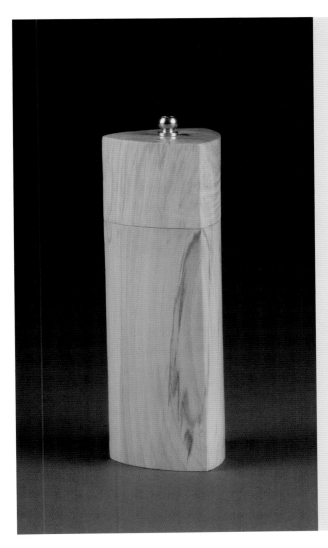

TOOLS
1 in. (25 mm) spindle roughing gouge
½ in. (13 mm) beading and parting tool
½ in. (13 mm) skew chisel
⅛ in. (3 mm) fluted parting tool
¾ in. (19 mm) Steb centre (toothed drive center)

Mechanism: 8 in. (203 mm) Type 1

WOOD
European sycamore

Height: 7⅝ in. (194 mm)
Diameter: 2¹¹⁄₁₆ in. (68 mm)
Blank dimensions: 3¼ x 3¼ x 9½ in. (82.5 x 82.5 x 241 mm)
These dimensions allow for facing off, waste, and tenons that will be removed as the project proceeds.

The design of this three-sided mill could hardly be simpler, but it brings an elegant variation to the traditional circular mill.

MARKING OUT THE BLANK
The key to a successful mill is very accurate measuring out at each end of the 9½ in. (241 mm) blank. Repeat steps 1–3 on page 124 at both ends of the blank. Keep the point numbers in line from one end to the other.

TURNING THE OUTSIDE
Mount the blank between a ¾ in. (19 mm) Stebcentre and the tailstock, using point 1 as the center at each end.

Initially, set the lathe to its lowest speed, then increase the speed gently, ensuring that the lathe is not vibrating or causing you undue

▶ **WARNING:**
Throughout the turning phase, keep revolving the blank by hand before turning on the lathe to check that the tool rest will not touch any of the three corners.

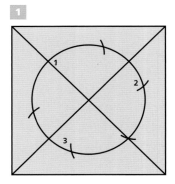

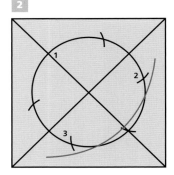

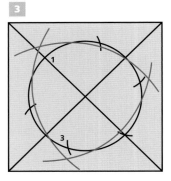

1 Draw the diagonals of your accurately squared blank.

Set your compass to a quarter of the length of the diagonal, which should come to 2⁷⁄₁₆ in. (62 mm), and draw a circle as shown.

Keeping the same compass radius, from point 1, walk round the circle, marking as you go, until you have divided the circumference into six equal parts. Mark points 2 and 3 as shown.

2 With the compass point at 1, draw an arc ⅛ in. (3 mm) less than the circle diameter.

3 Do the same from points 2 and 3. These three arcs show the finished shape of the mill.

stress. The only tool used for the turning of the mill's body and top is a 1 in. (25 mm) spindle roughing gouge. It is imperative that you keep checking that the blank does not touch the tool rest before starting to remove wood. Use light cuts as you move along the blank. The tool will often be cutting fresh air on this project! The speed can be increased by small increments as you remove the wood. Keep going until you are just short of the arcs marked on the ends. Using a metal ruler, check for evenness along the length. When you reach the arc lines, stop the lathe and hand-sand the convex curve using a block of cork or wood with abrasive paper wrapped round it, checking with a ruler that it is level as you go along.

Reposition the blank on the lathe so that each end is centered on point 2. Repeat the previous steps, then do the same with the ends centered on point 3.

BASE

When you are satisfied that the three convex curves are smooth, level, and equal, you can begin marking out of the length of the mill. Remount the mill between centers.

At the points where tenons are going to be cut and the waste removed from the bottom, it is advisable to wrap masking tape round the three sides before marking and cutting. This will help give you a clean cut at the corners and edges of the mill. Mark out and turn the two tenons as shown, then part the mill into two.

Mount the base by its tenon in compression jaws. When it is running true, bring up the tailstock for support. The ¼ in. (6 mm) of waste at the base of the mill is turned away using a ⅛ in. (3 mm) fluted parting tool. This removes the marks left by the Stebcentre.

The base can now be drilled as usual for a Type 1 mechanism.

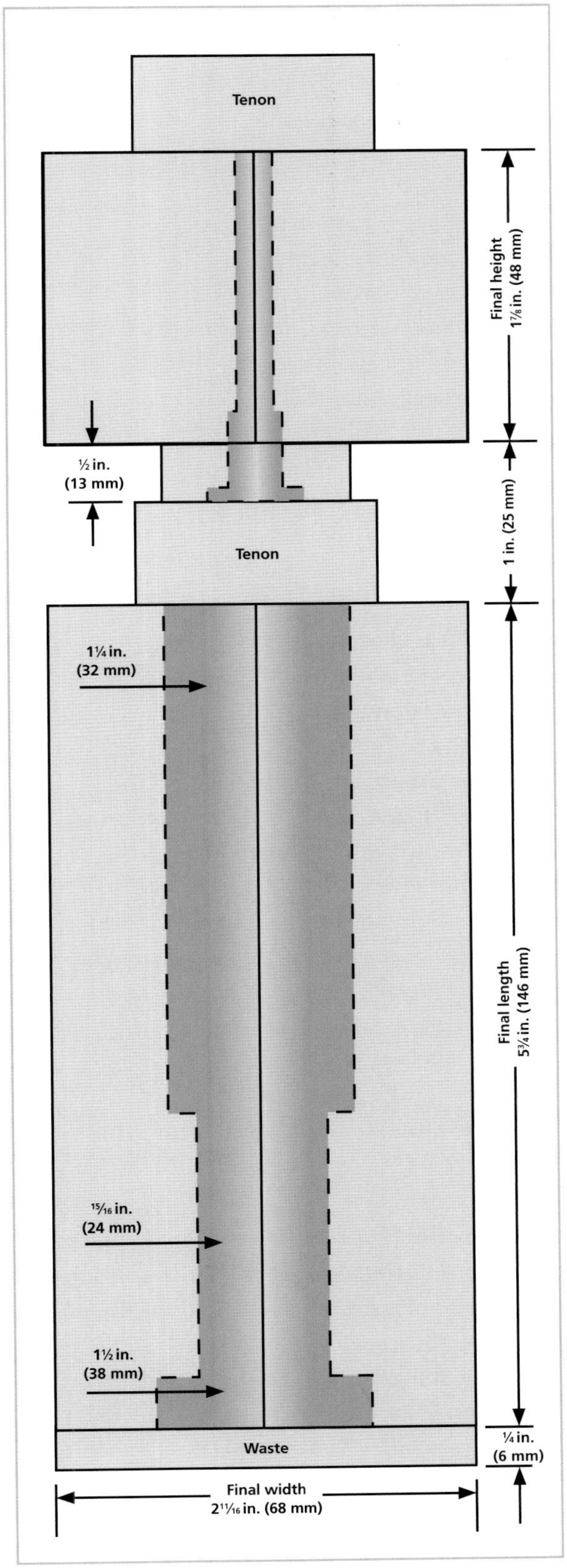

Diagram labels

Tenon

Final height
1⅞ in. (48 mm)

½ in.
(13 mm)

Tenon

1 in. (25 mm)

1¼ in.
(32 mm)

Final length
5¾ in. (146 mm)

1⁵⁄₁₆ in.
(24 mm)

1½ in.
(38 mm)

Waste

¼ in.
(6 mm)

Final width
2¹¹⁄₁₆ in. (68 mm)

Blank and finished mill layout

TOP

With the top held by its tenon in compression jaws, face off the spigot to approximately ⅜ in. (10 mm) long. Drill the two holes for the drive plug and the shaft hole to a depth of 1 in. (25 mm). Reduce the spigot diameter to fit into the 1¼ in. (32 mm) hole in the base. The fit should be loose without being sloppy, just enough to allow for any possible future movement of the wood. Mount the spigot in compression jaws and remove the tenon. The shaft hole is now drilled through and the top sanded and sealed in the usual way. The Type 1 drive plug and mechanism can now be fitted.

WHAT NEXT?

I would encourage you to try variations on three-sided shapes before moving on to *therming*, a traditional technique for making polygonal spindles. The lovely Teardrop mill by Dennis Cloutier shown in the Gallery on page 161 is a result of therming.

► **OTHER OPTIONS**

If you wish to fit a Type 2 mechanism, the following changes will be required:
• The blank will need to be longer.

• The grinding mechanism's hole will be a different diameter.

23 PALIO'S MILL

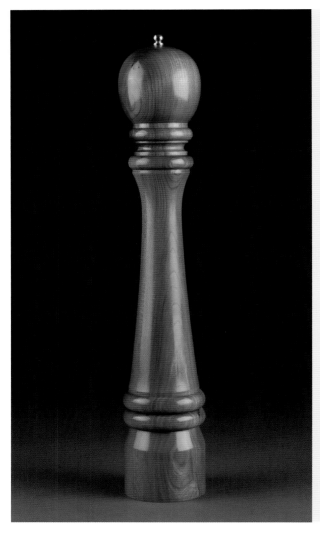

TOOLS
¾ in. (19 mm) spindle roughing gouge
⅜ in. (10 mm) spindle gouge
½ in. (13 mm) spindle gouge
½ in. (13 mm) beading and parting tool
½ in. (13 mm) skew chisel
⅛ in. (3 mm) parting tool

Mechanism: 20 in. (508 mm) Type 1

WOOD
English elm

Height: 20 in. (508 mm)
Diameter: 3⁹⁄₁₆ in. (90 mm)
Blank dimensions: 4 x 4 x 21 in.
(102 x 102 x 533 mm)
These dimensions allow for facing off the end grain surfaces and for the top's tenon or dovetail, which will be turned away as the project proceeds.
Note: If you do not have jumbo jaws to fit this 4 in. (102 mm) diameter mill, you will need to add ⅝ in. (16 mm) for a second tenon at the top of the base.

T his unusually tall design—a favourite with Italian restaurateurs—involves drilling the main reservoir from both ends using a sawtooth bit extension.

BASE

It is important that this very long base is held securely for drilling. To achieve this, the diameter of each end of the base should be of a size to accommodate jumbo jaws, while still leaving enough diameter to clean away markings left by the jaws.

The reservoir for the peppercorns needs to be around 14 in. (355 mm) in length. To achieve this depth, a sawtooth extension is used, which allows an extra 6 in. (150 mm) to be drilled.

Between centers, rough-turn and mark the key dimensions. Turn the required tenons and spigot, then saw or part off into two. Hold the top of the base in jumbo jaws (or by its tenon, if suitable jaws are not available) and ensure that it is running true. Face off the bottom, sand, and seal.

The 1½ in. (38 mm) hole for the grinding mechanism is drilled first, followed by the ¹⁵⁄₁₆ in. (24 mm) reservoir hole. Bore as far as the drill will allow without the extension. Keep the lathe speed at around 800 rpm for drilling, and withdraw the sawtooth bit every 1 in. (25 mm) to remove the shavings. If you don't, the bit will bind in the hole and prove very difficult to withdraw. You have been warned!

The next stage is to fit the 15/16 in. (24 mm) sawtooth bit into the extension and drill to half the length of the base. Again, withdraw the drill regularly to remove the shavings.

Reverse the base and, when it is running true, support with the tailstock to allow the base to be faced off to the correct length. The 1¼ in. (32 mm) hole for the spigot is drilled first, followed by the 15/16 in. (24 mm) sawtooth bit in the extension to complete the reservoir.

With the base mounted between a jam chuck and a cone center, shape the outside. After final shaping, sand down through the grits to 400.

TOP

With the tenon held in compression jaws, face off the spigot to a length of around ½ in. (13 mm). Drill the two holes for the drive plug and the shaft hole (see page 85) to a depth of 3 in. (76 mm).

Reduce the spigot diameter to fit the 1¼ in. (32 mm) hole in the base. This fit should, as usual, be loose without being sloppy. Shape the bottom half of the top, sand, and seal.

Remount, holding the spigot in compression jaws. Masking tape around the spigot will reduce marking. Remove the tenon when it is running true. The shaft hole is now drilled through and the top shaped. Sand and seal as before.

The Type 1 drive plug and the mechanism can now be fitted and the mill can be finished using your preferred method.

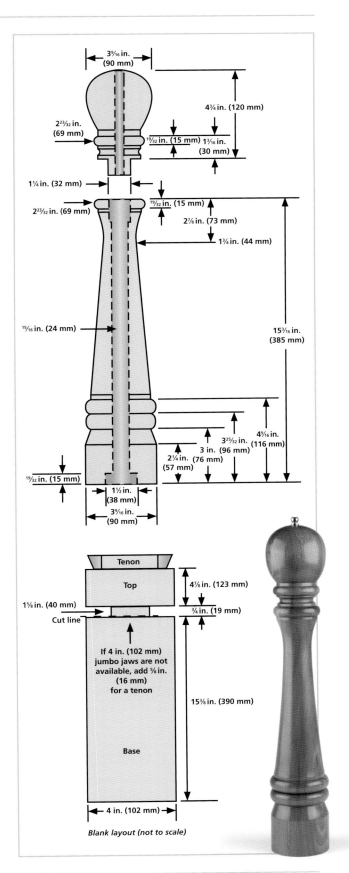

Blank layout (not to scale)

24 POCKET PEPPER MILL

Level of difficulty: **Intermediate**
(requires thread-chasing)

TOOLS

¾ in. (19 mm) spindle roughing gouge
⅜ in. (10 mm) spindle gouge
¼ in. (6 mm) spindle gouge
½ in. (13 mm) beading and parting tool
½ in. (13 mm) skew chisel
¹⁄₁₆ in. (1.5 mm) parting tool
½ in. (13 mm) round-nosed scraper
Recess tool
19 tpi thread chasers

Mechanism: 4 in. (102 mm) Type 1 with
shortened shaft

WOOD

Cocobolo

Height: 3³⁄₁₆ in. (81 mm)
Diameter: 2³⁄₁₆ in. (56 mm)
Blank dimensions: 2½ x 2½ x 5⅞ in.
(64 x 64 x 150 mm)
These dimensions include sufficient wood for
facing off and for tenons or dovetails.

This mill was inspired by the silver pocket-sized pepper mill used by DI Henry Crabbe in the British 1990s TV series *Pie in the Sky*. My design is meant to prevent the pepper falling out when it is kept in a waistcoat pocket!

This mill comes in three parts; the separate base has to be unscrewed to allow access to the pepper grinder itself.

BASE

Rough-turn the blank between centers and cut into three, as shown in the diagram. Mount the base by its tenon in your chuck jaws, with the tailstock in place to ensure that it is running true. Face off the base square. Shape and chase the female thread. The tenon will be turned off and the bottom finished later.

BODY

Mount the body by its tenon, face off, and chase the male thread. Drill the two holes for the mechanism but do not go all the way through with the ¹⁵⁄₁₆ in. (24 mm) drill. Screw the base onto the body and finish the bottom of the base; then remove the base.

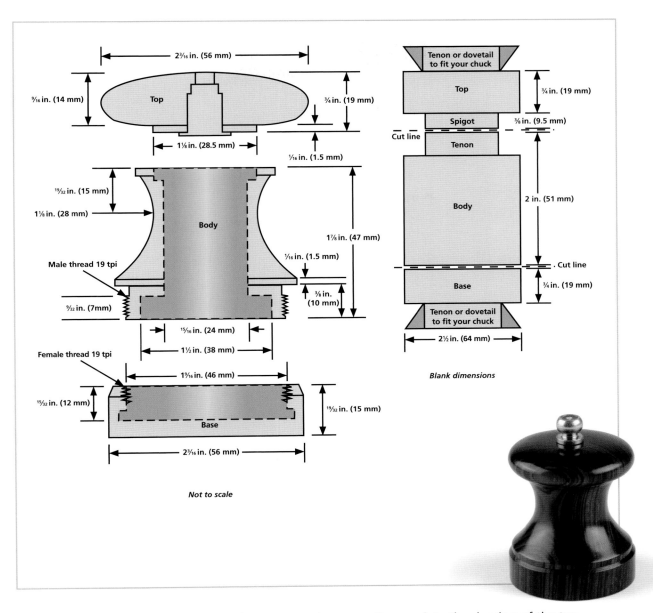

2³⁄₁₆ in. (56 mm)

⁹⁄₁₆ in. (14 mm)

Top

³⁄₄ in. (19 mm)

1⅛ in. (28.5 mm)

¹⁄₁₆ in. (1.5 mm)

¹⁹⁄₃₂ in. (15 mm)

1⅛ in. (28 mm)

Body

1⅞ in. (47 mm)

¹⁄₁₆ in. (1.5 mm)

Male thread 19 tpi

⁹⁄₃₂ in. (7mm)

³⁄₈ in. (10 mm)

¹⁵⁄₁₆ in. (24 mm)

1½ in. (38 mm)

Female thread 19 tpi

1⁹⁄₁₆ in. (46 mm)

¹⁵⁄₃₂ in. (12 mm)

¹⁹⁄₃₂ in. (15 mm)

Base

2³⁄₁₆ in. (56 mm)

Not to scale

Tenon or dovetail
to fit your chuck

Top

³⁄₄ in. (19 mm)

Spigot

³⁄₈ in. (9.5 mm)

Cut line

Tenon

Body

2 in. (51 mm)

Cut line

Base

³⁄₄ in. (19 mm)

Tenon or dovetail
to fit your chuck

2½ in. (64 mm)

Blank dimensions

Part off the body to its final length and reverse, holding the body by its bottom end in expansion jaws while you drill the two required holes from the top and shape the outside. For shaping, the body can be centered between a cone-shaped jam chuck and the tailstock.

TOP

Mount the top by its tenon and face off the spigot. Drill the drive plug's ¹¹⁄₃₂ in. (9 mm) hole to a depth of ⁹⁄₁₆ in. (14 mm). Turn the spigot to fit the body, then begin to shape the bottom curve. To complete the shaping of the top, reverse, holding the spigot in compression jaws to remove the tenon or dovetail, and finish shaping the top. Finally, drill the ⁵⁄₁₆ in. (8 mm) shaft hole.

Finish the mill using your preferred method. Shorten the shaft as described on pages 88–89 and fit the mechanism.

CRUSHGRIND® MECHANISM

DRILLING AND FITTING A CRUSHGRIND® MECHANISM

This section will take you through the steps required to drill the holes to take either the shaft or the wood versions of the CrushGrind® mechanism. I have assumed that you already have the blanks to make your mill.

There is no need to be apprehensive about using CrushGrind® mechanisms. Attention to detail and taking your time to get the drilling right will ensure a successful conclusion. However, the drilling instructions shown on the following pages are important. Be warned that if you do get this stage wrong, you may well find that the mechanism will not lock into position and that corrections cannot be made.

The diagram below shows a typical blank for a CrushGrind® shaft mechanism. The "spigot waste," around ⅝ in. (16 mm) long, provides a means of gripping the top if you wish to make a mill with the top turned off-center (as in the example by Brian Fitzsimmons in the Gallery, page 163); otherwise it will not be needed.

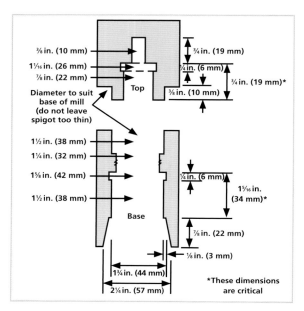

Drilling dimensions for shaft mechanism

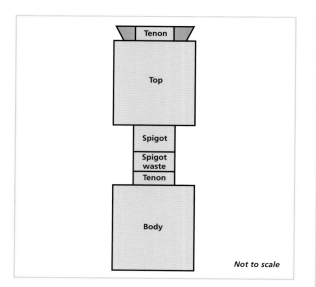

Layout of a typical blank to suit a CrushGrind® shaft mechanism

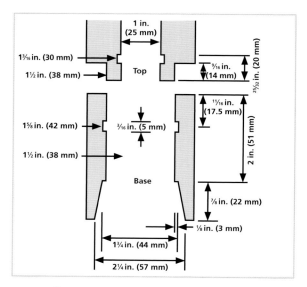

Drilling dimensions for a CrushGrind® wood mechanism

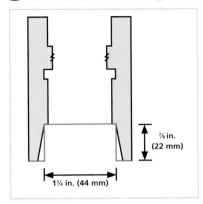

⁷⁄₈ in. (22 mm)

1¾ in. (44 mm)

1 Mount the top of the body in compression jaws. Partially tighten the jaws and ensure that the block is running true before tightening fully. With a 1¾ in. (44 mm) sawtooth bit, drill to a depth of ⁷⁄₈ in. (22 mm).

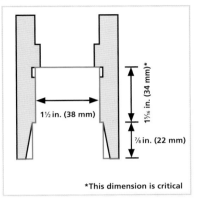

1⅝₁₆ in. (34 mm)*

1½ in. (38 mm)

⁷⁄₈ in. (22 mm)

*This dimension is critical

2 Time to concentrate now! Wrap masking tape around the shaft of a 1½ in. (38 mm) sawtooth bit, and mark with a pencil a depth of 2³⁄₁₆ in. (56 mm). (That is 1⁵⁄₁₆ in. or 34 mm more than the recess you have already drilled; if your first drilling was a little more or less than ⁷⁄₈ in. or 22 mm, take this into account.) After drilling, check with a depth gauge to ensure that this critical dimension is correct.

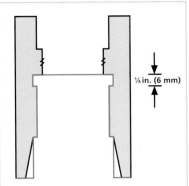

¼ in. (6 mm)

3 Next, turn the recess for the three lugs on the CrushGrind® mechanism, using a ¼ in. (6 mm) recess tool, supported by an armrest if you wish. The depth of cut should be a minimum of ⅛ in. (3 mm). The lathe should be running at around 1500 rpm.

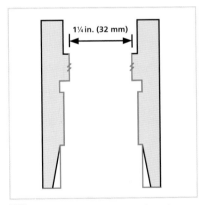

1¼ in. (32 mm)

4 Drill a 1¼ in. (32 mm) hole to a minimum depth of 2½ in. (64 mm) from the bottom end of the body.

5 Remove the base from the lathe. Either bandsaw the tenon off, or leave it until the work is mounted on the lathe again, when it can be taken off with a parting tool. Now change your chuck jaws to expansion jaws to fit the 1¾ in. (44 mm) diameter hole you have drilled.

6 Mount the base and, when you are satisfied it is running true, remove the tenon if you have not already done so, then bring up the tailstock for support. Mark out the desired length of the base, part off, sand, and seal.

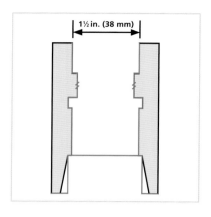

1½ in. (38 mm)

7 Remove the tailstock and prepare to drill a 1½ in. (38 mm)* hole to meet the 1¼ in. (32 mm) hole drilled earlier. Sand and seal the top face. Remove the work from the lathe.

You may choose to vary this diameter. It must match the diameter of the spigot in the top of the mill.

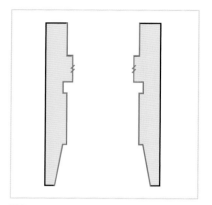

8 In order to give easy access to the mechanism adjusting nut, it is helpful to widen the lower end of the 1¾ in. (44 mm) hole. Mount the top end of the body in the expansion jaws and use a ½ in. (13 mm) skew to shape the opening. Take this opportunity to sand and seal the inside surface just formed.

DRILLING THE TOP

9 Hold the top by its tenon or dovetail in compression jaws. Ensure that it is running true. The following description assumes that you are not going to be needing the spigot waste shown in the first diagram on page 132. If you are intending to turn the top off-center, add the length of the waste to all the drilling depths shown.

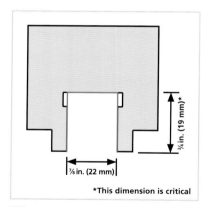

¾ in. (19 mm)*

⅞ in. (22 mm)

*This dimension is critical

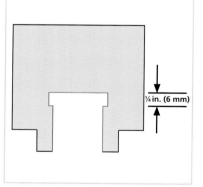

¼ in. (6 mm)

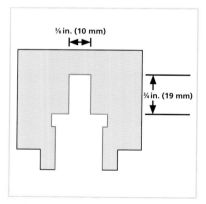

⅜ in. (10 mm)

¾ in. (19 mm)

10 Wrap tape around a ⅞ in. (22 mm) drill and mark a depth of ¾ in. (19 mm). Drill, ensuring that the depth is accurate.

11 Turn the recess for the three lugs on the CrushGrind® mechanism using a ¼ in. (6 mm) recess tool, supported by an armrest if you prefer. The depth of cut should be a minimum of ⅛ in. (3 mm). The lathe should be running at around 1500 rpm.

12 Finally, drill a ⅜ in. (10 mm) hole to a depth of ¾ in. (19 mm) to house the shaft.

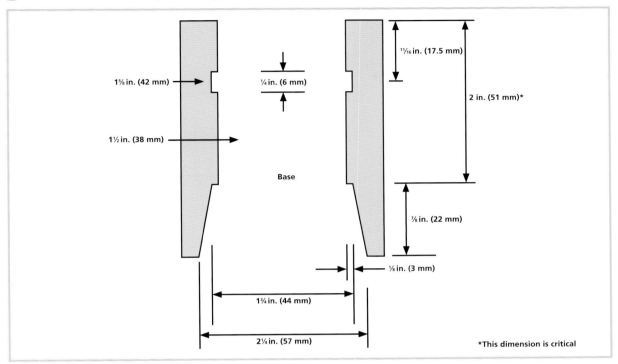

1⅝ in. (42 mm)
1½ in. (38 mm)
¼ in. (6 mm)
Base
¹¹⁄₁₆ in. (17.5 mm)
2 in. (51 mm)*
⅞ in. (22 mm)
⅛ in. (3 mm)
1¾ in. (44 mm)
2¼ in. (57 mm)
*This dimension is critical

1 Mount the tenon of the base in compression jaws. Loosely tighten the jaws and ensure that the block is running true before tightening fully. With a 1¾ in. (44 mm) sawtooth bit, drill to a depth of ⅞ in. (22 mm).

2 Drill right through the base using a 1½ in. (38 mm) sawtooth bit.

3 At the point where the two halves of the mechanism meet, there may be a raised piece of plastic. To eliminate the chance of this binding against the inside of the hole, approximately ⁵⁄₆₄ in. (2 mm) of wood should be removed around a point ¹¹⁄₁₆ in. (17.5 mm) from the top of the base. You should use either a ¼ in. (6 mm) recess tool or a curved side scraper.

4 Remove the base from the lathe. Either bandsaw the tenon off, or wait until it is mounted in the lathe again, when it can be taken off with a parting tool. Change your chuck jaws to a set of expansion jaws to fit the 1¾ in. (44 mm) diameter hole that is already drilled.

5 Mount the base and, when you are satisfied it is running true, bring up the tailstock for support. Mark out the desired length of the base, part off, sand, and seal.

6 In order to give easy access to the mechanism adjusting nut, it is necessary to widen the 1¾ in. (44 mm) hole. Mount the top of the base in the compression jaws and use a ½ in. (13 mm) skew to shape the opening. At this point, take the opportunity to sand and seal the bottom and the inside of the 1¾ in. (44 mm) hole.

Drilling the top

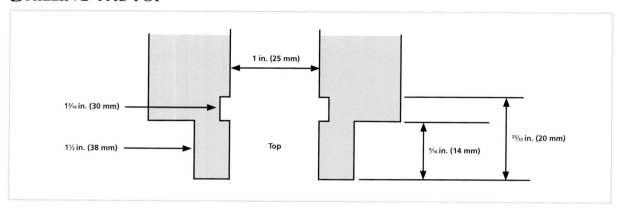

1 in. (25 mm)

1³⁄₁₆ in. (30 mm)

1½ in. (38 mm)

Top

⁹⁄₁₆ in. (14 mm)

²⁵⁄₃₂ in. (20 mm)

7 Hold the top by its tenon or dovetail in compression jaws. Ensure that it is running true. Face off the bottom of the spigot.

8 On a 1 in. (25 mm) drill, mark a depth of ²⁵⁄₃₂ in. (20 mm). Drill, ensuring that the depth is accurate.

9 Make the recess for the three lugs on the CrushGrind® mechanism using a ¼ in. (6 mm) recess tool, supported by an armrest, if preferred.

10 The final drilling will be 1 in. (25 mm) to a depth based on the design of your mill.

Note: When initially reducing the spigot diameter, make sure that it is a tight fit into the top hole of the base, prior to turning the outside of the mill. If you do not, the top will not run concentrically.

Fitting a CrushGrind® mechanism

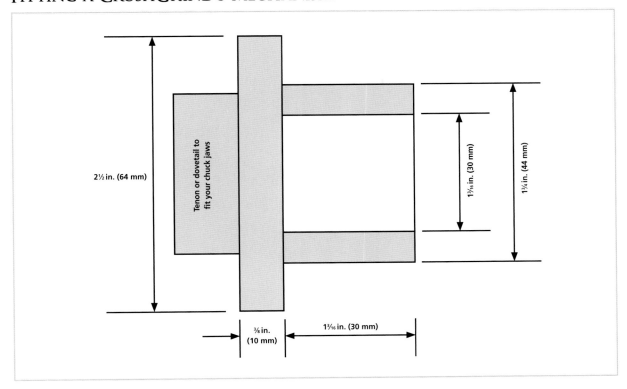

The best way to ensure that the grinding half of the mechanism is fitted squarely is to turn the jig shown in the diagram above. Then prepare a piece of planed hardwood approximately 5 x 3 x ½ in. (125 x 75 x 13 mm) with a ½ in. (13 mm) hole in its center. Place the jig in your compression jaws. Slip the top of the mechanism into the base of the mill and insert the bottom (the knurled nut end) into the 1³⁄₁₆ in. (30 mm) hole in the jig, placing the piece of hardwood between the tailstock barrel and the end of the mill base. Lock the tailstock in position. If you are fitting a shaft mechanism, the shaft of the mechanism may protrude through the hole, depending on the size of the spigot. Gently screw the tailstock against the piece of hardwood. The mechanism will be forced into the base and you will hopefully hear the springs click into the recess. If not, remove the mechanism and double-check your measurements—one of them is wrong!

Note: When fitting the main grinding part of the mechanism, *under no circumstances* should you try pressing or hammering against the gray knurled nut.

To fit the top half of the mechanism, the piece of hardwood can be used again. Working off the lathe, hold the mechanism in the drilled hole in the spigot, place the piece of hardwood against the base of the mechanism, and gently tap it in with a soft hammer, forcing the mechanism into the top. Again you should hear the lugs click in; if they don't, the top mechanism will come out when the top is pulled away from the base.

Shortening a CrushGrind® shaft

Having fitted both parts of the mechanism in place, push the top over the shaft as far as it will go. Measure the gap between the two halves of the mill; the shaft needs to be shortened by this amount, plus a further ⅛ in. (3 mm). Remove the excess using a hacksaw. Finally, file a chamfer on the top edges of the shaft.

To fit a CrushGrind® wood mechanism into the base and the top, use the same method.

MILL PROJECTS
(CrushGrind® mechanism)

25 MUSHROOM COMBO

■ Level of difficulty: **Intermediate**

TOOLS

¾ in. (19 mm) spindle roughing gouge
½ in. (13 mm) spindle gouge
½ in. (13 mm) beading and parting tool
³⁄₁₆ in. (5 mm) fluted parting tool
¾ in. (19 mm) skew chisel
⅛ in. (3 mm) parting tool
1 in. (25 mm) square-ended scraper
Recess tool with armrest

Accessories required: Several ⅞ in. (22 mm) internal diameter nitrile O-rings

Mechanism: 8 in. (203 mm) CrushGrind® shaft

WOOD

Masur birch

Height: 7⅜ in. (187 mm)
Diameter: 3⅛ in. (79 mm)
Blank dimensions:
Base: 3⅜ x 3⅜ x 6¼ in. (85 x 85 x 159 mm)
Top: 2⅜ x 4¾ x 4¾ in. (60 x 120 x 120 mm)
Spigot: 2⅜ x 2⅜ x 2½ in. (60 x 60 x 64 mm)
Plug: 1¾ x 1¾ x 1¾ in. (44 x 44 x 44 mm)

A combo or two-in-one mill allows pepper to be ground from one end and salt shaken out at the other. This design is based on my mother's sock-darning mushroom. It looks a little different, but at times you have to let your imagination come into play!

There are three separate pieces to this mill, because the spigot between the body and top is made as a separate insert; you will also need to turn a plug for the salt shaker. The key to the design is that the top is cross-grained. The shaft of the 8 in. (203 mm) CrushGrind® shaft mechanism will have to be reduced for this project. Refer to pages 133–134 for details of the drill sizes and order of drilling. If you are planning to design and turn a number of

CrushGrind® mills, it is recommended that you copy the drilling dimensions for the two types of mechanisms, shown on pages 132–136.

I cannot stress strongly enough the importance of careful measurement with these CrushGrind® projects. Once the mechanisms have been pushed into place there is little chance of you being able to remove them without causing damage to both the mill and the mechanism.

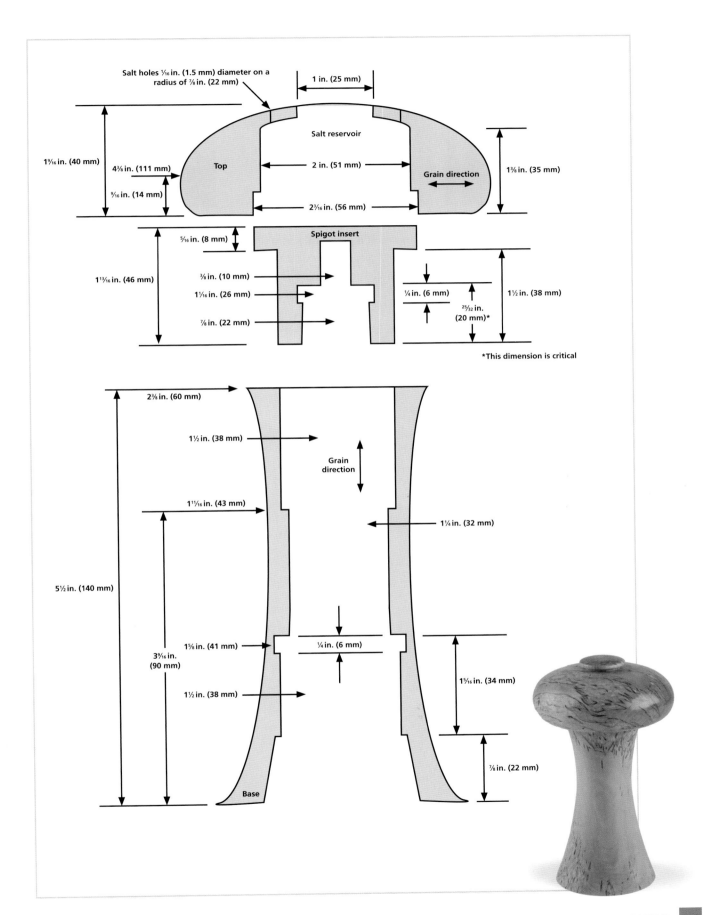

Salt holes ¹⁄₁₆ in. (1.5 mm) diameter on a
radius of ⁷⁄₈ in. (22 mm)

1 in. (25 mm)

Salt reservoir

1⁹⁄₁₆ in. (40 mm)

4³⁄₈ in. (111 mm)

Top

2 in. (51 mm)

Grain direction

1³⁄₈ in. (35 mm)

⁹⁄₁₆ in. (14 mm)

2³⁄₁₆ in. (56 mm)

⁵⁄₁₆ in. (8 mm)

Spigot insert

1¹³⁄₁₆ in. (46 mm)

³⁄₈ in. (10 mm)

1¹⁄₁₆ in. (26 mm)

⁷⁄₈ in. (22 mm)

¼ in. (6 mm)

1½ in. (38 mm)

²⁵⁄₃₂ in.
(20 mm)*

*This dimension is critical

2⅜ in. (60 mm)

1½ in. (38 mm)

Grain
direction

1¹¹⁄₁₆ in. (43 mm)

1¼ in. (32 mm)

5½ in. (140 mm)

3⁹⁄₁₆ in.
(90 mm)

1⅝ in. (41 mm)

¼ in. (6 mm)

1⁵⁄₁₆ in. (34 mm)

1½ in. (38 mm)

⁷⁄₈ in. (22 mm)

Base

BASE

1 Mount the blank between centers, rough out and turn the tenon or dovetail to fit your chuck. Remove from the lathe.

2 Insert the tenon in compression jaws and bring up the tailstock. Ensure that the work is running true. Face off the bottom of the base, making it slightly concave. Drilling for the mechanism can now be started: see pages 132–134 for details. Accuracy is paramount.

3 After drilling the 1¾ in. (44 mm) and 1½ in. (38 mm) holes to the correct depth, make the recess using the recess tool. The hole in the base will be widened later. Drill the 1¼ in. (32 mm) hole to a depth of approximately 3¾ in. (95 mm).

4 Remove from the lathe, reverse, and mount the base in expansion jaws. Mark out the length of the base and face off. Now drill a 1½ in. (38 mm) hole to meet the existing hole. All of the drilling of the base is now complete and the base is ready for shaping.

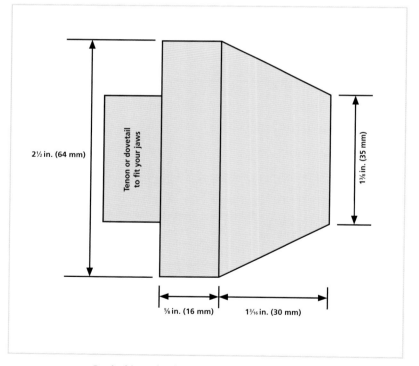

2½ in. (64 mm)

Tenon or dovetail to fit your jaws

1⅜ in. (35 mm)

⅝ in. (16 mm)

1³⁄₁₆ in. (30 mm)

Conical jam chuck to support base (see step 5)

5 A conical jam chuck is recommended to support the base when turning its outside shape. The base of the mill is held between the chuck and the tailstock.

6 Shape the outside using a ½ in. (13 mm) spindle gouge. In order to give easy access to the mechanism's adjusting nut, it is helpful to widen the 1¾ in. (44 mm) hole. Mount the top end of the base in the expansion jaws and, when running true, use a ½ in. (13 mm) skew to shape the opening. This is a good opportunity to sand through the grits to 400. Stopping the lathe and sanding horizontally between grits will improve the finish.

Top

7 Rough out between centers, allowing some waste in both the length and the diameter of the top, and turn either a tenon or a dovetail at the top end.

Remove from the lathe and remount with the tenon in compression jaws. Clean up the bottom face using a 1 in. (25 mm) square scraper. Using either a pencil or dividers, mark a 2⁷⁄₃₂ in. (56 mm) circle on the bottom face.

8 Open up this hole to a depth of ⁵⁄₁₆ in. (8 mm) to form the recess for the spigot. Then, using either a 2 in. (51 mm) diameter Forstner bit or a ½ in. (13 mm) beading and parting tool, open the hole to a depth of 1⅜ in. (35 mm) for the salt reservoir. The objective is to try to leave ³⁄₁₆ in. (5 mm) thickness for the plug at the top.

9 Reduce the outside diameter of the top to slightly more than the 4⅜ in. (111 mm) that is required. Mark the positions of the bottom curve as shown in the diagram and use either a ⅜ in. (10 mm) or a ½ in. (13 mm) gouge to round off the curve, as shown.

10 To complete the curve of the top, change to expansion jaws and hold the top by the 2³⁄₁₆ in. (56 mm) recess hole.

11 This is a good time to mark out the circumference on which the salt holes will be drilled. Place masking tape over the area where the holes will be drilled and draw a circle of ⁷⁄₈ in. (22 mm) radius.

Remove the top from the lathe. Decide how many salt exit holes you want and drill them using a drill press and a ¹⁄₁₆ in. (1.5 mm) drill bit. Return the mill top to the lathe, as in step 10, and drill the 1 in. (25 mm) hole into the reservoir for the salt plug.

SPIGOT INSERT

12 Rough out the blank between centers and turn a tenon on the top surface to fit your lathe jaws. Hold the tenon in compression jaws while you face off the base of the spigot.

13 Referring to the main diagram and page 134 for details, drill the necessary mechanism holes in the top. Use a recess tool, as in step 11 on page 134, to make the slot for the spring clips on the mechanism.

14 Turn down the diameter of the spigot to 1½ in. (38 mm) using a ½ in. (13 mm) beading and parting tool. As you near the final diameter, test the fit with the base of the mill. You are aiming for a loose fit, but not sloppy. When you're done, remove the work from the lathe.

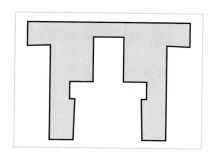

15 Wrap the spigot in masking tape before holding in compression jaws (or use plastic jaws). After ensuring it is running true, turn the top end of the spigot to fit snugly into the mill top. Do not glue it into the mill top until the salt plug has been turned and fits perfectly; this allows for any alterations to the thickness of the wood around the hole for the salt plug.

SALT PLUG

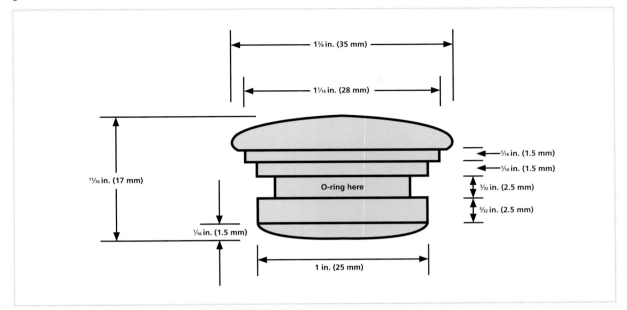

1⅜ in. (35 mm)

1¹⁄₁₆ in. (28 mm)

¹¹⁄₁₆ in. (17 mm)

O-ring here

¹⁄₁₆ in. (1.5 mm)
¹⁄₁₆ in. (1.5 mm)
³⁄₃₂ in. (2.5 mm)
³⁄₃₂ in. (2.5 mm)

¹⁄₁₆ in. (1.5 mm)

1 in. (25 mm)

16 Mount the blank between centers and turn a tenon on one end. Remove from the lathe. Holding it in compression jaws, turn the bottom end of the plug down to 1 in. (25 mm), as shown. Leave extra length if your tailstock is supporting the end. Allowing at least ⁹⁄₃₂ in. (7 mm) thickness for the rounded top, turn the small ¹⁄₁₆ in. (1.5 mm) shoulder at the bottom.

Now is the time to be both patient and careful. Turn the slot for the rubber O-ring—hopefully you will have bought enough O-rings to keep testing the fit into the top of the salt reservoir. You will find that the O-rings expand and sometimes split when put on the plug a number of times. When you can fit the salt plug easily into the top and it does not fall out when upturned, you are there.

Remove the O-ring. If you have plastic jaws, fit these to your chuck; if not, wrap some masking tape round the partially turned plug and grip in compression jaws while you finish turning the top curve.

ASSEMBLY

The spigot insert can now be glued into the mill top using the tailstock as a support. When dry, sand off any roughness from drilling the salt holes. Remove from the lathe.

For fitting instructions, refer back to page 137. Measure and shorten the shaft of the mechanism using a hacksaw and file.

FINISHING

All that is left to do now is to finish the mill to your requirements. Mine was sprayed with an acrylic gloss lacquer. Further information on this can be found on page 25.

VARIATIONS

From this basic design, mills can be made using either Type 1 or Type 2 traditional mechanisms. A separate spigot insert will not be required—the top blank should be deep enough to incorporate the spigot.

26 Chess King

■ Level of difficulty: **Intermediate**

Tools
¾ in. (19 mm) roughing gouge
½ in. (13 mm) spindle gouge
½ in. (13 mm) beading and parting tool
³⁄₁₆ in. (5 mm) fluted parting tool
½ in. (13 mm) skew chisel
⅛ in. (3 mm) parting tool

Mechanism: 8 in. (203 mm) CrushGrind® shaft

Wood
False acacia

Height: 9⅛ in. (232 mm)
Diameter: 3⁹⁄₁₆ (90 mm)
Blank dimensions: 4 x 4 x 11 in.
(102 x 102 x 280 mm)

In this design, the recess for the mechanism is formed within the top itself, not in the spigot. This method allows the use of a narrow spigot, giving additional flexibility to your designs.

Mount the blank between centers, rough-turn, mark out the key dimensions, and turn the tenon and spigot. Part off at the point shown.

Base
Mount the tenon in compression jaws and center it. Face off the bottom of the base. Drill for the mechanism as described on pages 132–134.

Mount the base between centers using a conical jam chuck and the tailstock, and shape the outside.

Top
Hold the tenon in compression jaws. Turn the spigot to its correct length of ¹³⁄₃₂ in. (10 mm) and diameter of 1⁵⁄₃₂ in. (29 mm) so it will fit easily into the hole in the base.

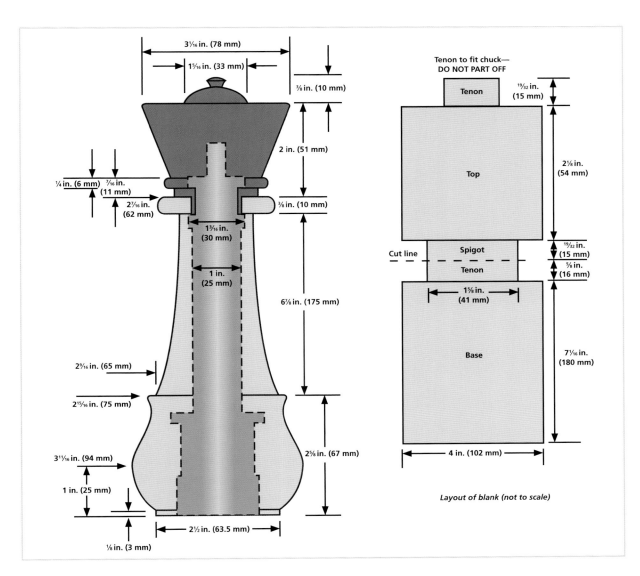

3¹/₁₆ in. (78 mm)
1⁵/₁₆ in. (33 mm)
³/₈ in. (10 mm)
2 in. (51 mm)
¼ in. (6 mm)
⁷/₁₆ in. (11 mm)
2⁷/₁₆ in. (62 mm)
³/₈ in. (10 mm)
1³/₁₆ in. (30 mm)
1 in. (25 mm)
6⁷/₈ in. (175 mm)
2⁹/₁₆ in. (65 mm)
2¹⁵/₁₆ in. (75 mm)
2⁵/₈ in. (67 mm)
3¹¹/₁₆ in. (94 mm)
1 in. (25 mm)
2½ in. (63.5 mm)
⅛ in. (3 mm)

Tenon to fit chuck—
DO NOT PART OFF
Tenon
¹⁹/₃₂ in. (15 mm)
Top
2⅛ in. (54 mm)
Cut line
Spigot
¹⁹/₃₂ in. (15 mm)
Tenon
⅝ in. (16 mm)
1⅝ in. (41 mm)
Base
7¹/₁₆ in. (180 mm)
4 in. (102 mm)

Layout of blank (not to scale)

Drill the holes for the mechanism as shown on page 132.

Reverse, holding the spigot in compression mode. *Do not remove the tenon*; this becomes the dome at the very top of the mill. Shape the outside, sand, and seal.

FITTING THE MECHANISM

If your lengths are correct, you should not have to shorten the shaft. If it does not fit, either drill the top shaft hole deeper or remove the excess shaft with a hacksaw and clean up the top edges with a file. Follow the assembly instructions on page 137.

FINISHING

Finish the mill using one of the methods discussed on pages 22–25.

27 DECANTER

TOOLS
¾ in. (19 mm) spindle roughing gouge
½ in. (13 mm) spindle gouge
½ in. (13 mm) beading and parting tool
³⁄₁₆ in. (5 mm) fluted parting tool
¾ in. (19 mm) skew chisel
⅛ in. (3 mm) parting tool

Mechanism: 8 in. (203 mm) CrushGrind® shaft with shortened shaft

WOOD
Yew

Height: 10 in. (255 mm)
Diameter: 4 in. (102 mm)
Blank dimensions:
Mill: 4⅛ x 4⅛ x 10⅝ in. (105 x 105 x 270 mm)
Stopper: 1¾ x 1¾ x 3 in. (44 x 44 x 76 mm)
These dimensions allow for facing off and for tenons or dovetails that will be removed as the work proceeds.

This mill is operated by twisting the neck of the decanter. The stopper is purely for decoration and is glued into the top of the mill.

Turn to a cylinder between centers. Mark out the key dimensions and turn the tenons, dovetail and spigot as required. Part the base from the top while still between centers, or cut apart on a bandsaw.

BODY
Insert the tenon in compression jaws and center the work. Face off the bottom of the body. Then drill the first holes for the mechanism, working from the base, as described on pages 133–134.

With the tailstock in place, start roughing out the bottom half. Reverse and remount in expansion jaws, face off to the correct length and drill the remaining holes. Rough-shape the top half.

TOP
Hold the tenon in compression jaws. Drill the holes necessary for the mechanism, as shown on page 134. Turn the spigot to its correct length and diameter, making it a tight fit in the mill body at this stage.

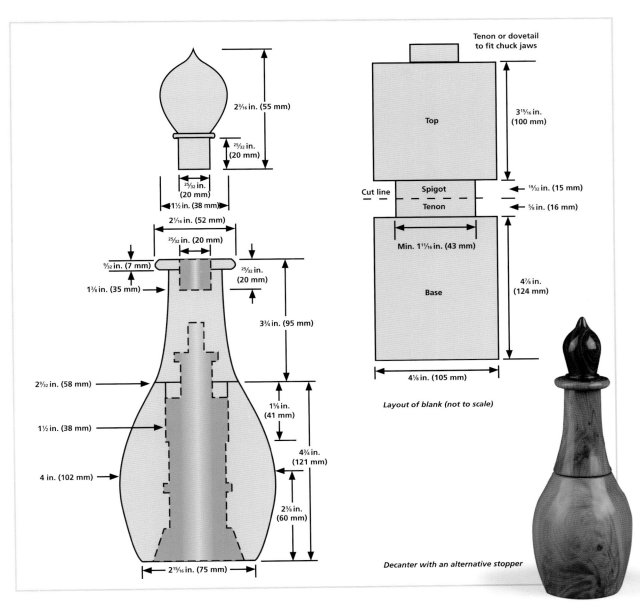

2³⁄₁₆ in. (55 mm)

²⁵⁄₃₂ in. (20 mm)

²⁵⁄₃₂ in. (20 mm)

1½ in. (38 mm)

2¹⁄₁₆ in. (52 mm)

²⁵⁄₃₂ in. (20 mm)

⁹⁄₃₂ in. (7 mm)

1³⁄₈ in. (35 mm)

²⁵⁄₃₂ in. (20 mm)

3¾ in. (95 mm)

2⁹⁄₃₂ in. (58 mm)

1½ in. (38 mm)

4 in. (102 mm)

1⁵⁄₈ in. (41 mm)

4¾ in. (121 mm)

2³⁄₈ in. (60 mm)

2¹⁵⁄₁₆ in. (75 mm)

Tenon or dovetail to fit chuck jaws

Top

3¹⁵⁄₁₆ in. (100 mm)

Cut line

Spigot

Tenon

¹⁹⁄₃₂ in. (15 mm)

⁵⁄₈ in. (16 mm)

Min. 1¹¹⁄₁₆ in. (43 mm)

Base

4⁷⁄₈ in. (124 mm)

4¹⁄₈ in. (105 mm)

Layout of blank (not to scale)

Decanter with an alternative stopper

Reverse, holding the spigot in compression mode, remove the tenon, and part off the top to its correct length. Drill the ²⁵⁄₃₂ in. (20 mm) hole for the stopper.

Fit the two halves of the mill together and, using a jam chuck and the tailstock for support, complete the shaping of the outside. Sand and seal. Remount and reduce the diameter of the spigot to give ample room for the top to turn in the base without sticking.

STOPPER

Turn the stopper to a shape of your choosing. The material can be colored, textured, or plain. Rough out to a cylinder between centers and turn a ²⁵⁄₃₂ in. (20 mm) spigot. Hold this in compression mode, and turn and finish the stopper before gluing it into the top of the mill.

FITTING THE MECHANISM

Work out the length of shaft you require. Remove the excess with a hacksaw and clean up the top edges of the shaft with a file. Follow the fitting instructions on page 137. All that remains is to finish the mill to your requirements.

28 CHEWED PEAR

■ Level of difficulty: **Intermediate**

TOOLS
¾ in. (19 mm) spindle roughing gouge
½ in. (13 mm) spindle gouge
½ in. (13 mm) beading and parting tool
⅛ in. (3 mm) parting tool

Mechanism: CrushGrind® wood

WOOD
English walnut

Height: 5½ in. (140 mm) without the stalk
Diameter: 4 in. (101 mm)
Blank dimensions:
Mill: 4⅛ x 4⅛ x 7¾ in. (105 x 105 x 197 mm)
Stalk: 1⅜ x 1⅜ x 2¾ in. (35 x 35 x 70 mm)
These dimensions allow for facing off and
for tenons or dovetails.

I t's not unheard of for turners to seek inspiration from fruit—and it needn't even be a whole fruit! This mill uses a tapered plug (stalk) in the top for filling with pepper.

Rough out between centers and turn the top tenon or dovetail to fit your chuck. Mark the key dimensions and the grain direction on each half, and part off into two sections.

BODY
Hold the tenon in compression jaws. Ensure that it is running true and bring up the tailstock. Face off the bottom of the mill. Drill the holes necessary for the mechanism, as detailed on pages 135–136.

Hold the bottom of the body in expansion jaws. Mark out the body length and face off. Widening of the hole in the base will be completed after turning the outside.

TOP
Hold the tenon in compression jaws. Refer to page 136 for drilling instructions and drill the 1 in. (25 mm) hole to a depth of 2 in. (51 mm). Turn the spigot to its correct length and diameter, making it a tight fit into the base at this stage.

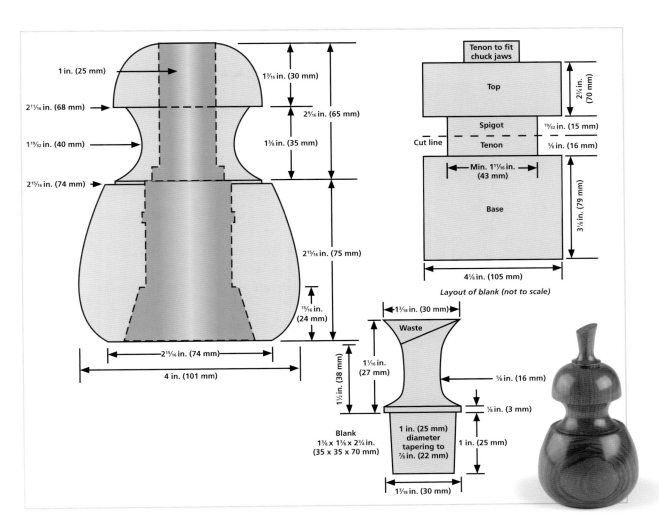

1 in. (25 mm)

2¹¹⁄₁₆ in. (68 mm)

1¹⁹⁄₃₂ in. (40 mm)

2¹⁵⁄₁₆ in. (74 mm)

1³⁄₁₆ in. (30 mm)

2⁹⁄₁₆ in. (65 mm)

1⅜ in. (35 mm)

2¹⁵⁄₁₆ in. (75 mm)

¹⁵⁄₁₆ in. (24 mm)

2¹⁵⁄₁₆ in. (74 mm)

4 in. (101 mm)

Tenon to fit chuck jaws

Top

2¾ in. (70 mm)

Spigot

¹⁹⁄₃₂ in. (15 mm)

Cut line

Tenon

⅝ in. (16 mm)

Min. 1¹¹⁄₁₆ in. (43 mm)

Base

3⅛ in. (79 mm)

4⅛ in. (105 mm)

Layout of blank (not to scale)

1³⁄₁₈ in. (30 mm)

Waste

1¹⁄₁₆ in. (27 mm)

⅝ in. (16 mm)

⅛ in. (3 mm)

1½ in. (38 mm)

Blank
1⅜ x 1⅜ x 2¾ in.
(35 x 35 x 70 mm)

1 in. (25 mm) diameter tapering to ⅞ in. (22 mm)

1 in. (25 mm)

1³⁄₁₈ in. (30 mm)

Reverse the top, holding the spigot in compression mode. Remove the tenon and part the top to its correct length. Drill the 1 in. (25 mm) hole to meet the existing one. Fit the two halves of the mill together, and, using a conical jam chuck and the tailstock for support, shape the outside. Remount the top between the jam chuck and the tailstock and reduce the diameter of the spigot slightly.

Remove from the lathe and hold the top half of the base in expansion jaws. When running true, widen the opening at the bottom of the base enough to allow easy access to the knurled nut on the mechanism.

FILLING PLUG

The pear-stalk plug is made from walnut. Either rough out and shape between centers, or turn a tenon and hold it in compression mode for

shaping. The stalk top is angled using a table sanding disk or any other suitable means available to you. Alternatively, you could make a simple plug like that used in the Mushroom project (page 145, step 16). The dimensions given there will fit this project too.

FINAL STAGES

Fit the mechanism as instructed on page 137, and apply the finish of your choice.

▶ **VARIATIONS**

Similar mills could be turned using traditional mechanisms, either Type 1 or Type 2. The pear's stalk could have an insert nut fitted to replace the supplied finial nut. You would need to shorten the shaft.

29 CHESS PAWN

■ Level of difficulty: **Experienced**

TOOLS

¾ in. (19 mm) spindle roughing gouge
½ in. (13 mm) and ¾ in. (19 mm) spindle gouges
¾ in. (19 mm) skew chisel
¹⁄₁₆ in. (1.5 mm) and ⅛ in. (3 mm) parting tools
½ in. (13 mm) beading and parting tool
1 in. (25 mm) square-ended scraper
Recess tool and armrest
Template with 1½ in. (38 mm) concave curve

Mechanism: CrushGrind® shaft

WOOD

Ash; masur birch for the ring top; ebony for the stem through the ring

Height: 11 in. (280 mm)
Diameter: 3⅛ in. (80 mm)
Blank dimensions:
Body: 3⅜ x 3⅜ x 8¼ in. (85 x 85 x 210 mm)
Top: 1¹³⁄₁₆ x 3⅛ x 5 in. (46 x 80 x 127 mm)
Top shaft: ¹³⁄₃₂ x ¹³⁄₃₂ x 4 in. (10 x 10 x 102 mm)

The top of this mill introduces a completely different shape, and one that takes some care to turn. The holes for the top section of the mechanism are all included within the spigot.

BODY

Mount the blank between centers and rough-turn. Prepare and drill for the CrushGrind® shaft mechanism as described on pages 133–134. With the work mounted between a conical jam chuck and the tailstock, begin shaping the outside using a ¾ in. (19 mm) spindle gouge. After final shaping, sand down through the grits to 400, until you are happy that there are no sanding marks. I chose to ebonize and add gold gilt cream to my mill, using the method on page 22.

TOP

The blank should have edges and sides flat at 90° to each other. Accurately mark the center of each end. Draw a line along one face between the centers and mark the position of the 1⅜ in. (35 mm) central hole, which is centered 2¹¹⁄₁₆ in. (68 mm) from the spigot end (excluding waste for facing off). Drill the hole. Mount the blank between centers with the spigot end at the headstock. Turn to a diameter of 2¾ in. (70 mm). At the tailstock end, turn a tenon to fit your compression jaws.

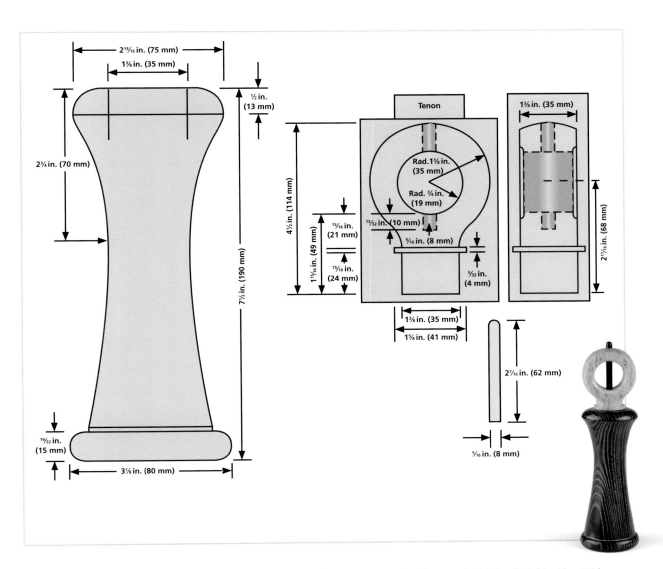

Remount the tenon in compression jaws. Measure 1¹⁵⁄₁₆ in. (49 mm) from the bottom edge of the hole; this point will be the end of the spigot. All measurements on the diagram are made from this point. Face off the spigot and drill the holes for the top of the CrushGrind® mechanism, as described on page 134. Turn the spigot to fit into the base, and turn the ⁵⁄₃₂ in. (4 mm) collar.

Make up a template with a 1⅜ in. (35 mm) radius internal curve. Remount the spigot in compression jaws and remove the tenon. Using the template, turn the outside of the ring to blend into the collar step. Drill a ⁵⁄₁₆ in. (8 mm) hole through the top of the ring to a depth of ¹³⁄₃₂ in. (10 mm) into the other side. Now is the time to be 100% focused—your knuckles will be close to the projecting spigot as the work rotates.

Use expansion jaws to hold the finial by the 1⅜ in. (35 mm) hole while you reduce the width of the top to 1⅜ in. (35 mm). Use the outside of the ⁵⁄₁₆ in. (8 mm) hole to measure a distance of ¹⁷⁄₃₂ in. (13.5 mm) to the outside of the top.

Use a 1 in. (25 mm) square-end scraper very carefully to reduce the width of the ring. Reverse the work and repeat for the other side. I turned a rounded chamfer on each inner edge of the 1⅜ in. (35 mm) hole. Sand the finial and apply the finish as you wish.

Turn a stem with one end rounded over, 2⁷⁄₁₆ in. (62 mm) long by ⁵⁄₁₆ in. (8 mm) diameter. This can be ebonized sycamore or ebony itself. Glue this into the ring. Finally, install the CrushGrind® shaft mechanism, as described on page 137.

30 DOUBLE-ENDED

TOOLS

1 in. (25 mm) spindle roughing gouge
⅜ in. (10 mm) and ½ in. (13 mm) spindle gouges
½ in. (13 mm) beading and parting tool
½ in. (13 mm) skew chisel
⅛ in. (3 mm) parting tool
Recess tool

Accessories required: Several ⅞ in. (22 mm) internal diameter nitrile O-rings

Mechanism: Two CrushGrind® wood mechanisms

WOOD

Ash; yew and ebony inserts

Height: 10 in. (254 mm)
Diameter: 3⅛ in. (80 mm)
Blank dimensions:
Body: ash, 3⁹⁄₁₆ x 3⁹⁄₁₆ x 12 in. (90 x 90 x 305 mm)
Contrasting rings: yew and ebony, each 2⅜ x 2⅜ x ⅝ in. (60 x 60 x 15 mm)
Filler plugs: yew and ebony, each 1⅜ x 1⅜ x 2 in. (35 x 35 x 51 mm)

This mill uses two CrushGrind® wood mechanisms to grind salt at one end and pepper at the other. The outside shape is very simple. I hope this project will spark your imagination to try other interesting shapes and woods. The turning is relatively straightforward; it's accurate drilling that's important.

The mill body is made from four blocks, of which 1 and 4, and 2 and 3, are identical. These are all cut, before turning begins, from a single length of ash. Number the four pieces and draw an arrow on each one pointing toward the center of the mill, to ensure that the grain runs continuously through the whole length of the mill and any attractive figure is preserved.

BLOCKS 1 AND 4

Mount block 1 between centers so that the end with the arrowhead is at the tailstock end. Reduce the diameter to 3⅜ in. (85 mm). Face up at the tailstock end first, removing the minimum amount, then measure back 2¾ in. (70 mm) and face off the other end. This ensures that the maximum amount of matching grain remains next to block 2. Make sure both ends are square.

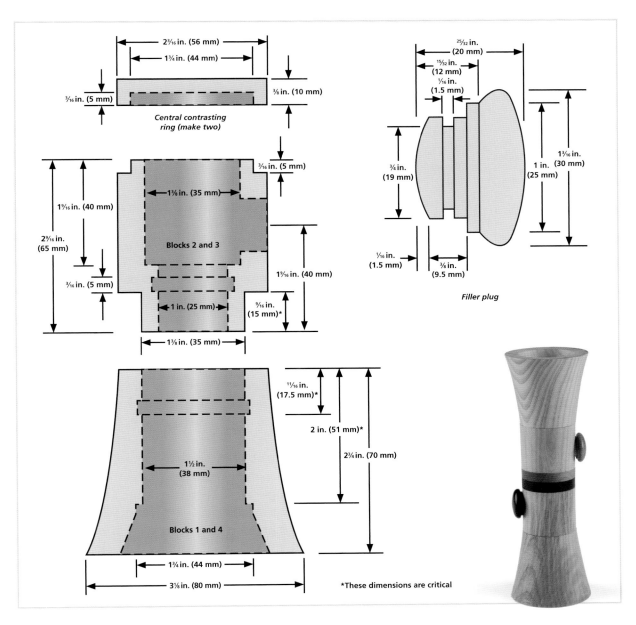

Central contrasting
ring (make two)

2³⁄₁₆ in. (56 mm)

1¾ in. (44 mm)

³⁄₁₆ in. (5 mm)

³⁄₈ in. (10 mm)

Blocks 2 and 3

1⅜ in. (35 mm)

³⁄₁₆ in. (5 mm)

1⁹⁄₁₆ in. (40 mm)

2⁹⁄₁₆ in. (65 mm)

³⁄₁₆ in. (5 mm)

1 in. (25 mm)

1⁵⁄₁₆ in. (40 mm)

⁹⁄₁₆ in. (15 mm)*

1⅜ in. (35 mm)

²⁵⁄₃₂ in. (20 mm)

¹⁵⁄₃₂ in. (12 mm)

¹⁄₁₆ in. (1.5 mm)

³⁄₄ in. (19 mm)

1³⁄₁₆ in. (30 mm)

1 in. (25 mm)

¹⁄₁₆ in. (1.5 mm)

³⁄₈ in. (9.5 mm)

Filler plug

Blocks 1 and 4

1½ in. (38 mm)

1¾ in. (44 mm)

3⅛ in. (80 mm)

¹¹⁄₁₆ in. (17.5 mm)*

2 in. (51 mm)*

2¾ in. (70 mm)

*These dimensions are critical

Redraw the arrow, facing right, to make sure you know which end to make the tenon, which is part of the top of blocks 1 and 4. Remember that the headstock end is the base of the mill, so you need your tenon at the tailstock end, to fit your compression jaws.

Mount the blank by its tenon in compression jaws, with the arrow towards the headstock, and drill for the mechanism as described on page 135. Repeat for block 4. Watch out for the arrow orientation.

Jam chuck and drive tenons

This is a good opportunity to make the jam chuck and the two drive tenons shown overleaf.

Contrasting rings

The yew and ebony blanks should be square. Find the exact center by drawing diagonals on both sides and center-punching. Mount one piece between centers and true up both faces. The thickness does not matter at this stage, as long as it is more than ¹⁵⁄₃₂ in. (12 mm). Repeat for the second piece.

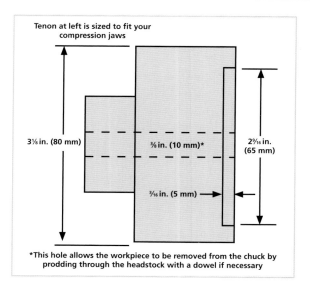

Tenon at left is sized to fit your compression jaws

3⅛ in. (80 mm)

⅜ in. (10 mm)*

2⁹⁄₁₆ in. (65 mm)

³⁄₁₆ in. (5 mm)

*This hole allows the workpiece to be removed from the chuck by prodding through the headstock with a dowel if necessary

Jam chuck (make one)

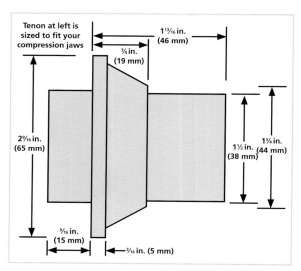

Tenon at left is sized to fit your compression jaws

1¹³⁄₁₆ in. (46 mm)

¾ in. (19 mm)

2⁹⁄₁₆ in. (65 mm)

1½ in. (38 mm)

1¾ in. (44 mm)

⁹⁄₁₆ in. (15 mm)

³⁄₁₆ in. (5 mm)

Drive tenon (make two)

Hold each piece in turn in a vise, and drill a 1¾ in. (44 mm) hole ¼ in. (6 mm) deep.

Return to the lathe and mount between centers again. Turn each piece to approximately 2½ in. (65 mm) diameter. Do your best to make both the same diameter; this helps when you come to put them in the jam chuck.

Place the first piece into the jam chuck with its drilled side facing out. True up the face until the depth of the hole is ³⁄₁₆ in. (5 mm). Repeat for the other piece.

Check how deep the pieces fit into the jam chuck. Insert one piece into the jam chuck with the flat side facing you. Knowing the depth of the jam chuck, make a pencil mark on the piece to give you ¹³⁄₃₂ in. (10 mm) overall length. Ensure that the new face is absolutely true. This face is going to be glued to the other piece, so you don't want to see any gaps between the two.

Now glue the two pieces together on their flat surfaces. Insert the drilled side of one piece into the jam chuck. Glue with the grain of the two pieces at 90° to each other and bring the tailstock up for support. I used a two-part epoxy adhesive.

BLOCKS 2 AND 3

While still square, mark out the blocks for the ¾ in. (19 mm) filler plug holes; because these will be on opposite sides of the finished mill, one of the blocks will need to be turned through 180° to keep the grain orientation correct before drilling. Drill on a drill press to a depth of 1½ in. (38 mm).

Mount block 2 between centers so that the end with the arrowhead faces the tailstock. Rough-turn the wood down to around 2⅜ in. (60 mm) diameter, or whatever will fit your compression jaws. Redraw the arrow pointing to the tailstock. Measure 1⁹⁄₁₆ in. (40 mm) from the center of the hole to the face at the base of the arrow (headstock end). Clean up this face, then measure from this face 2⁹⁄₁₆ in. (65 mm) and true up the second face.

Now mount the end with the arrowhead in compression jaws. Ensure that the block is running true. Drill a 1 in. (25 mm) hole 1½ in. (38 mm) deep. Mark on the recess tool a line ²⁵⁄₃₂ in. (20 mm) from its end, and use it to make a slot ³⁄₁₆ in. (5 mm) deep at this point.

Measure ¹⁹⁄₃₂ in. (15 mm) from the tailstock face and turn a spigot down to around 1½ in. (38 mm) diameter. Offer block 1 to the spigot; keep reducing it until you have a tight fit. This will ensure that all four blocks turn concentrically.

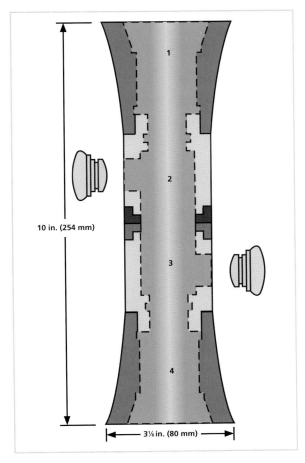

General arrangement of the parts

Push in blocks 1 and 4 and, using your two drive tenons as support, mount the whole assembly between centers while you shape and finish the outside of the mill.

Remove from the lathe and take off blocks 1 and 4. Remount block 2 in compression jaws, using the tailstock center at the other end. Relieve the spigot on block 3 to allow for a free turning action. Turn the assembly end for end and repeat for the spigot of block 2.

FILLER PLUGS

Turn the two filler plugs as shown in the diagram. You may need to adapt the depth of the slot to fit the O-rings you have. Do remember to buy more O-rings than you need, as they are likely to get damaged when you pull them on and off to check the fit.

FINAL STAGES

The completed mill can now be remounted using the two drive tenons and then finished to your preference.

To assist fitting the mechanism into blocks 1 and 2, use one of the drive tenons. This fits over the screw in the CrushGrind® mechanism and allows it to be tapped into the base. You should be able to push the CrushGrind mechanism into blocks 2 and 3 by hand.

Turn the block around and hold the spigot in the compression jaws. Ensure that it is running true. Drill a 1⅜ in. (35 mm) hole 1⁹⁄₁₆ in. (40 mm) deep. Turn a step, ³⁄₁₆ in. (5 mm) wide, down to a diameter of 1¾ in. (44 mm). Offer one of the contrasting rings to this tenon to ensure a good fit before gluing. Decide which ring will eventually be glued to this block, and make a note of it.

Repeat these steps for block 3.

ASSEMBLY

Glue blocks 2 and 3 to the central rings, making sure that the two plug holes are 180° apart. I temporarily put dowels in each hole so that I could see that the two sections were at 180° to each other. If the drilling was correct, the grain should also line up.

> **HINT:**
> If the grain is pronounced and you want to preserve as much of it as possible, then instead of forming the bottom tenon from block 2, you can make up a separate tenon from hardwood and drill, fit, and glue it into block 2.

GALLERY

DENNIS CLOUTIER

Dennis strives to produce simple, elegant forms that are also functional. He has placed work in several shows, including the American Association of Woodturners' *Turned For Use II*.

For the past 10 years, Dennis has divided his time between production woodturning and engineering. He lives with his wife, Kerry, also a woodturner, and two golden retrievers near Vancouver, Canada.

They have a website at **www.runningdogwoodworking.com**

Quilted pepper mill
Quilted bigleaf maple

Height: 11 in. (280 mm)
Diameter: 3 in. (76 mm)

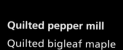

Teardrop pepper mill

Curly bigleaf maple

Height: 11 in. (280 mm)
Diameter: 2–3½ in. (51–89 mm)

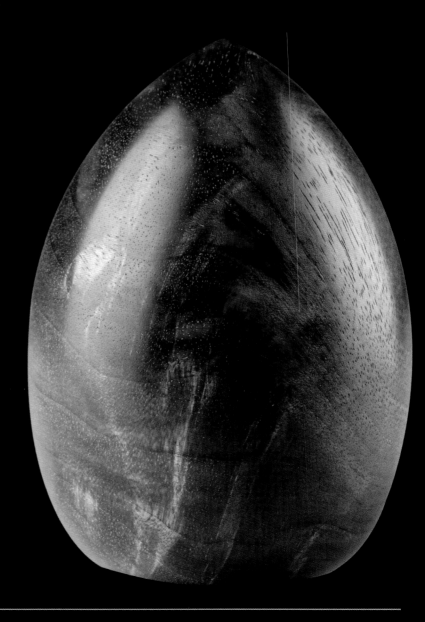

Salt shaker

Claro walnut

Height: 4 in. (101 mm)
Diameter: 2½ in. (64 mm)

BRIAN FITZSIMMONS

Brian is an innovative turner whose mills are very popular when they appear in shows, mainly in his home county of Suffolk, UK.

When Brian isn't woodturning he can usually be found fishing for trout with a dry fly on the chalk streams of southern England. He lives with his long-suffering wife, Valerie, who has nothing to do with wood. She feels that looking after him is more than enough!

Brian is proud of the fact that it was he who introduced CrushGrind® to the UK woodturning market some years ago, and he is still the sole agent for the sale of mechanisms by Cole & Mason.

He has a website at
www.peppergrinders.co.uk

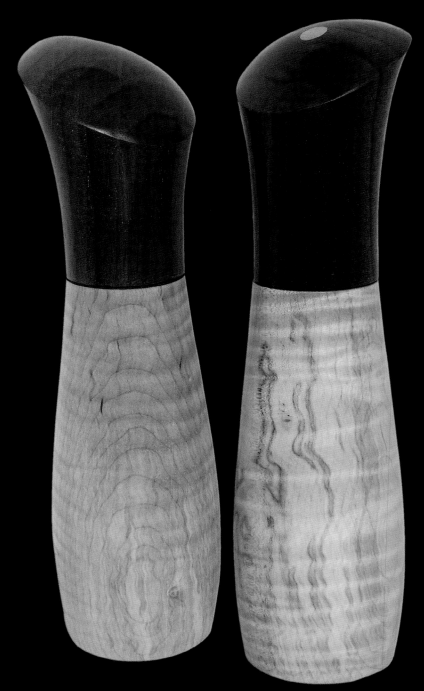

Pepper mills
Ripple maple, with American black walnut tops

Height: 11 in. (275 mm)
Diameter: 3 in. (75 mm)

GARY RANCE

Gary is known as one of the
best spindle turners around.
He has traveled throughout the
UK, Europe, and North America
demonstrating his skills.

His website is at
www.garyrance.co.uk

Pair of pepper mills
Oak

Height: 10½ in. (267 mm)
Diameter: 3 in. (75 mm)

CHRIS WEST

When designing new shakers and mills, Chris tries to think outside the box, incorporating new materials into his condiments—including metals, as shown on the next page.

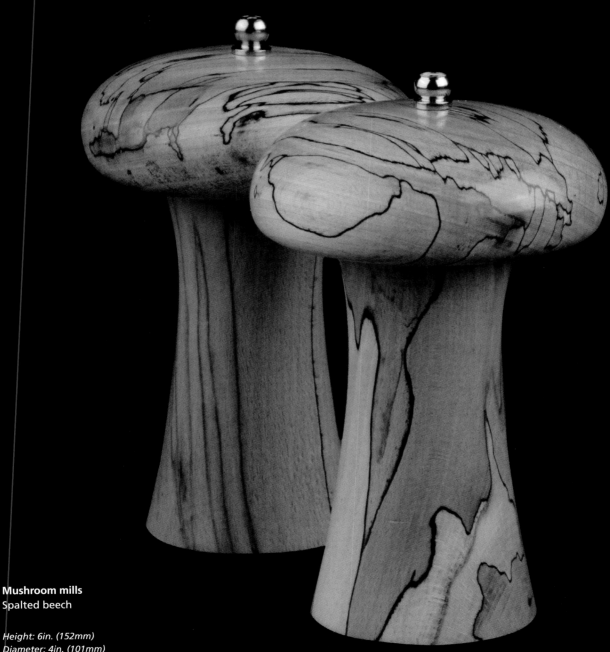

Mushroom mills
Spalted beech

Height: 6in. (152mm)
Diameter: 4in. (101mm)

Beer bottle salt and pepper mills
Ebonized sycamore finished
with gloss acrylic lacquer

Height: 9 in. (228 mm)
Diameter: 2¾ in. (70 mm)

 # SUPPLIERS

This list is not exhaustive; there may be other excellent suppliers that I am unaware of. Please note that, although mill mechanisms are available in a wide range of sizes, individual suppliers may not stock the full range; it is advisable to check with your chosen supplier before ordering.

USA AND CANADA

Craft Supplies USA
www.woodturnerscatalog.com
Tel. +1-800-551-8876
Chef Specialties (Type 2) salt and pepper mill mechanisms; salt-shaker caps

Lee Valley Tools Ltd.
www.leevalley.com
Tel. (from USA) +1-800-871-8158
Tel. (from Canada) +1-800-267-8767
Type 2 salt and pepper mill mechanisms

Packard Woodworks Inc.
www.packardwoodworks.com
Tel. +1-800-683-8876
Type 2 salt and pepper mill mechanisms

Rockler Woodworking and Hardware
www.rockler.com
Tel. +1-800-279-4441
Type 2 salt and pepper mill mechanisms; synthetic finishing pads

Woodcraft Supply
www.woodcraft.com
Tel. +1-800-225-1153
Type 2 salt and pepper mill mechanisms; salt-shaker tops; plastic plugs

UK

Altec Products Ltd.
www.altecweb.com
Tel. +44 (0)845 359 9000
O-rings

Axminster Power Tool Centre Ltd.
www.axminster.co.uk
Tel. +44 (0)800 371822
Synthetic finishing pads

Chestnut Products
www.chestnutproducts.co.uk
Tel. +44 (0)1473 425878
Chestnut finishing products

Constable Woodcrafts
www.peppergrinders.co.uk
Tel. +44 (0)1206 299400
Cole & Mason (Type 1) and CrushGrind® mechanisms; Type 1 bullet finial nuts

Craft Supplies Ltd.
www.craft-supplies.co.uk
Tel. +44 (0)1433 622550
CrushGrind® mechanisms; rubber bungs

Crafty Computer Paper Ltd.
www.craftycomputerpaper.co.uk
Tel. +44 (0)1434 689153
Decals and labels (supplies worldwide)

John Davis Woodturning
www.johndaviswoodturning.co.uk
Tel. +44 (0)1264 811070
CrushGrind® mechanisms;
synthetic finishing pads;
polyester resin blocks

WestWood Turnery (Chris West)
www.westwoodturnery.co.uk
Tel. +44 (0) 1794 512718
Slotted-screw finial nuts (Types 1 and 2);
insert nuts (Types 1 and 2)

Phil Irons Woodturning
www.philirons.com
Tel. +44 (0)1789 204052
CrushGrind® mechanisms; MillDrill™

NEW ZEALAND
Woodcut Tools Ltd.
www.woodcut-tools.com
Tel. + 64 (0) 6 875 1066
CrushGrind®; MillDrill™

AUSTRALIA
Some suppliers of CrushGrind® mechanisms

Carroll's Woodcraft Supplies (Victoria)
www.cws.au.com
Tel. +61 (0) 3 5251 3874

The Woodsmith Pty Ltd (Victoria)
www.thewoodsmith.com.au
Tel. +61 (0) 3 9722 9663

Pop's Shed (Victoria)
www.popsshed.com.au
Tel. +61 (0) 3 9727 0611

Macwood International (South Australia)
Tel. +61 (0) 8 8363 4666
www.macwood.com.au

Wood N Workshop (Queensland)
Tel. +61 (0) 7 5493 5069
www.woodnworkshop.com.au

CONVERSION CHART

INCHES	CENTIMETERS	MILLIMETERS
1/32	0.08	0.8
1/16	0.16	1.6
3/32	0.23	2.3
1/8	0.3	3
5/32	0.4	4
3/16	0.48	4.8
7/32	0.56	5.6
1/4	0.6	6
9/32	0.71	7.1
5/16	0.79	7.9
11/32	0.87	8.7
3/8	1.0	10
1/2	1.3	13
5/8	1.6	16
23/32	1.82	18.2
3/4	1.9	19
25/32	1.98	19.8
13/16	2.06	20.6
27/32	2.14	21.4
7/8	2.2	22
29/32	2.3	23

INCHES	CENTIMETERS	MILLIMETERS
15/16	2.38	23.8
31/32	2.46	24.6
1	2.5	25
1 1/4	3.2	32
1 1/2	3.8	38
1 3/4	4.4	44
2	5.1	51
2 1/2	6.4	64
3	7.6	76
3 1/2	8.9	89
4	10.2	102
4 1/2	11.4	114
5	12.7	127
6	15.2	152
7	17.8	178
8	20.3	203
9	22.9	229
10	25.4	254
11	27.9	279
12 1/2	30.5	305

FURTHER READING

Baker, Mark, **Wood for Woodturners**
(Lewes: GMC Publications, 2004)
ISBN 978-1-86108-324-6

Darlow, Mike, **Woodturning Design**
(Ammanford: Stobart Davies, 2002)
ISBN 978-0-85442-096-4

Edlin, Herbert L., **What Wood Is That?
A Manual of Wood Identification**
(Ammanford: Stobart Davies, 2009)
ISBN 978-0-85442-008-7

Gardiner, Julie, and Allen, Michael J. (eds.),
**Before the Mast: Life and Death Aboard
the Mary Rose**
(Portsmouth: Mary Rose Trust, 2005)
ISBN 978-0-95440-294-5

Levi, Jonathan, and Young, Robert,
**Treen for the Table: Wooden Objects
Related to Eating and Drinking**
(Woodbridge: Antique Collectors Club, 1998)
ISBN 978-1-85149-284-4

McConnell, Andy, **The Decanter: An Illustrated
History of Glass from 1650**
(Woodbridge: Antique Collectors Club, 1999)
ISBN 978-1-85149-428-6

Perlson, Mark, **Danish Pepper: Jens Quistgaard's
Teak Pepper Mills**
(San Francisco: Mark Perlson, 2008)
ISBN 978-1-438214-74-0

Van den Bossche, Willy, **Antique Glass Bottles:
Their History and Evolution, 1500–1850**
(Woodbridge: Antique Collectors Club, 1999)
ISBN 978-1-85149-337-1

ACKNOWLEDGMENTS

To my wife Kath, who always knew I was in one of two places during the writing of this book: in the workshop, or in front of the computer. Many thanks for your patience. I promise I will now get on with the items on the Things to Do list.

My thanks go to Ian Woodford and Ian Holdsworth, who took their red pens to my early text sections. Their advice and constructive criticism were appreciated.

Throughout the writing of the book, Brian Fitzsimmons was always on hand to give technical advice on Type 1 and CrushGrind® mechanisms.

Thanks to the Mary Rose Trust for the photograph of the 16th-century mill brought up from the *Mary Rose*.

A big thank you to Gary Rance for the Foreword. Gary, you are an inspiration for all spindle turners throughout the world.

Thanks to Stephen Haynes for the great job he has done on editing the book, and to Anthony Bailey for the beautiful photographs he has taken.

Thanks to Gary Rance, Dennis Cloutier, and Brian Fitzsimmons for allowing me to feature their turned shakers and mills in the Gallery.

Throughout the writing of this book, I have received great encouragement, support, and advice on condiment uses in North America from two good friends in Tucson, Arizona: David and Denise Liberis. Many thanks.

The support and advice given to me by Lynda McIntyre on some of the photographic work in the book was very much appreciated.

I thank Craft Supplies USA and Constable Woodcrafts for their help with information about their products.

PICTURE CREDITS

Photographs in this book are by Anthony Bailey, art-directed by Rob Janes © GMC Publications Ltd 2011, with the following exceptions:
Chris West pp14–16, 31, 82–83; Kathleen West, pp44–45, 94–97; Dennis Cloutier pp159–162; Brian Fitzsimmons pp163; GMC pp165–167; Istockphoto p26; Mary Rose Trust, Portsmouth p29; The Garlic Farm, Newchurch, Isle of Wight p30; Quidi Vidi Brewery, St John, Newfoundland p31 [photo of beer bottle].

Diagrams by Robin Shields and Rob Janes.

ABOUT THE AUTHOR

Although he has attended numerous demonstrations given by professional turners, Chris West describes himself as a self-taught club turner who has been enjoying his craft for over 30 years. During the last dozen or so, Chris has specialized in making salt and pepper mills and shakers.

On leaving school, Chris started his career in the computer industry, serving a five-year apprenticeship as an electromechanical engineer—yes, computers had moving parts in those days! One aspect of his job was the need to work within tight tolerances. This gave Chris the necessary skills for turning matching pairs of mills.

He remained in the industry until he took early retirement, and now spends a good deal of his time in his workshop. Chris's schedule also includes taking his woodturning experience to "outside" groups by giving talks to interested social organizations.

Many of Chris's mills have appeared in GMC's *Woodturning* magazine, and he hopes that by producing this book he can share his knowledge and experience with many budding and experienced woodturners.

Chris is an active member of the Hampshire Woodturners Association (HWA), the Test Valley Turners (TVT), and the American Association of Woodturners (AAW).

INDEX

To place an order or to request a catalogue, contact:
GMC Publications Ltd.
Castle Place, 166 High Street, Lewes, East Sussex, BN7 1XU, United Kingdom
Tel: +44 (0)1273 488005   Fax: +44 (0)1273 402866   www.gmcbooks.com